Praise for *Night Fishing*

'In this "natural history" of the author herself, we travel gently
through childhood and family, grief, love and solitude—and her
spellbinding twin obsessions with art and the natural world. It is
the work of a questing, roving intellect and a rare humility, and
Hastrich's sheer joy in language infuses the whole with a deliciously
sly, intelligent humour. I'd liken her to an antipodean Annie Dillard
with a fishing rod in one hand and the whole of western art history
in the other—except there simply is no other writer like Hastrich.
This book will tell you things you never knew about
your world and yourself, and you will never forget it.'
Charlotte Wood, author of *The Natural Way of Things*

'I read *Night Fishing* in one greedy gulp, marvelling at its
intelligence, humour, beauty and wonder. Immediately I'd finished,
I began again, reading each meticulous essay with care, taking my
time, wanting—needing—to attend to the words in the way that
Vicki Hastrich attends to her world. She sees every overlooked
detail. She listens for the quiet thrum under the everyday. She
invites us, via great art or small fish, into the depths of her
remarkable and unique world view. Her personal vision is both
intimate and epic. Every essay relates an episode observed and
considered with writerly precision and delicacy. *Night Fishing* is
a unique memoir from a powerful, tender and insightful writer.
It's the book I want everyone I love to read. It's a book I will never
let go. Vicki Hastrich depicts a life lived with eyes and mind wide
open. She even made me w
Ailsa Piper, co-author of

'Loved this—a gentle, meditative surge, a memoir which never strays too far from that big collective unconscious, the sea. Here the sea is night-fear, is stumps in the water mistaken for doughty swimmers, is secrecy, is revelation. On the journey, there are pearls—a mother doing crosswords in an austere billiard table showroom, and so passing the ocean of words to her daughter; the numbfish, a death harbinger; Galileo painting the waxing and waning moon as the world's water heaves from its pull; *Dasyatis brevicaudata* caught in the Garden Island graving dock, destined to glide out their graceful days in the Taronga Park Aquarium. And childhood, the most sparkling and scary sea of all.'

@tomsbooks

Praise for *The Great Arch*

'I gulped down *The Great Arch* in two long sittings, cancelling a coffee date because I didn't want to put it down. Hastrich had me hooked from the opening pages . . . I feel like climbing the bridge and yelling out how good it is.'

Christos Tsiolkas, author of *The Slap*

'. . . a story of imagination, loneliness, obsession and love . . . A deeply tender, very funny and sad and beautiful book.'

Charlotte Wood, author of *The Children*

'. . . as airy, soaring and magnificent as the bridge itself.'

Michelle de Kretser, author of *The Lost Dog*

Praise for *Swimming with the Jellyfish*

'Seemingly effortless, completely endearing, this novel is an absolute joy.'
Debra Adelaide, *The Sydney Morning Herald*

'. . . dazzling in its surprising juxtapositions of human types and in its colloquial flashes . . .'
Michael Sharkey, *The Australian*

'A deceptively clever first novel.'
Ian McFarlane, *The Canberra Times*

VICKI HASTRICH is a Sydney writer. She started out with the ABC as a TV camera operator and became an assistant director in drama. When she began writing, a range of jobs followed, including warehouse hand, picture researcher, factory worker, archivist and oral historian. Along the way she picked up a Doctor of Arts degree from the University of Sydney. Her two novels, *Swimming with the Jellyfish* and *The Great Arch*, were published in 2001 and 2008 respectively. She has recently turned to non-fiction. 'Things Seen', a cornerstone essay in *Night Fishing*, was first published in *The Best Australian Essays 2016*.

VICKI HASTRICH

NIGHT
FISHING

STINGRAYS, GOYA AND
THE SINGULAR LIFE

A MEMOIR IN ESSAYS

ALLEN&UNWIN
SYDNEY•MELBOURNE•AUCKLAND•LONDON

Australian Government

Australia | **Council**
for the Arts

This project has been assisted
by the Australian government
through the Australia Council,
its arts funding body.

Allen & Unwin
83 Alexander Street
Crows Nest NSW 2065
Australia
Phone: (61 2) 8425 0100
Email: info@allenandunwin.com
Web: www.allenandunwin.com

NATIONAL
LIBRARY
OF AUSTRALIA

A catalogue record for this
book is available from the
National Library of Australia

ISBN 978 1 76087 550 3

Set in 12.5/18 pt Fairfield LT by Midland Typesetters, Australia
Printed and bound in Australia by Griffin Press, part of Ovato

10 9 8 7 6 5 4 3 2

For Di
We're going to Woy Woy.

'. . . *the sea is the first home of the mind* . . .'
Peter Godfrey-Smith, *Other Minds*

Contents

The Hole

I learnt the word 'trespass' at an early age. Not from Sunday school, although I heard it there—*forgive us our trespasses*—but from signs hung on oyster leases.

Trespassers will be prosecuted.

In my head this meant they would be shot. Crazy Shackleton had a gun and we believed he'd use it. Reach a hand in through the watery fence line of any of the leases he farmed and he'd blow your head off.

Shackleton lived in a closed-up cottage behind a rank wall of lantana and morning glory. Angry dogs to match their angry master barked from somewhere out the back but were never seen. Shackleton was not much seen himself—at least by me. But those signs were everywhere. Also: *Keep out.* Some were hand-painted and some stencilled, but whether the

1

lettering was industrial or mad and fierce, they fairly screamed: *Mine, mine.*

Somehow they made the place even better. And, oh God, that place was good.

We went to this spot on the New South Wales Central Coast on semi-regular holidays with my parents' best friends and their three children. Uncle Clive and Aunty Pam, as they were to us, co-owned the house with Clive's sister-in-law. His mother had bought the water-access-only house on the Brisbane Water estuary in the 1930s. It was four rooms, had no electricity or running water, and was furnished with stuff that would already have been old in the thirties, a few key pieces of which were particularly alluring to us kids: a gramophone player the size of a fridge and six records, five of which we broke; a piano, out of tune, with hinged brass candlesticks that folded out either side of a music ledge; and a medicine cabinet full of strange little jars and bottles—ipecac, gentian violet and ointments ancient enough to have come from a pharaoh's tomb, all of it probably lethal. There were many kerosene lamps of various shapes and sizes on a shelf in the kitchen; on the same shelf was an alarm clock made out of a tuna tin. In the front room there were holes in the floorboards that one could lie down beside and put an eye to; dark shapes in the gloom included that of a claw-footed bath. Thankfully we washed in a big enamelled basin placed on the kitchen floor, because the idea of bathing in the dark under the house was beyond terrifying.

No one would do it nowadays—take six kids, food, ice and pets (including, once, a labrador with ten puppies and our mean cat) across the water in a hired putt-putt boat, haul the lot up a rough track to a dilapidated cottage on a hill, there to lie on kapok mattresses and poo on a can dunny while batting off pterodactyl-sized mozzies—and call it fun. Probably nobody else did it much then either; after all, it was the swinging sixties and Australia was getting modern.

I loved it. We all did. But I *really* loved it.

I was the youngest child in our family and I remember, before I even went to school, trailing around behind my mum as she did the housework in our nice new suburban home, plaintively, pathetically, whining, 'When are we going to Woy Woy?' That was the catch-all name we gave to the area and you can imagine how well those two syllables lent themselves to being drawn out by a whingey kid. I felt I was being unfairly kept away from my rightful life. I should live there. I might consent to go to school when the time came, if I could go by ferry.

Most mornings up there, the dads took the kids fishing in the boat; that is, after enough swearing and pulling on the leather strap cranked the flywheel and the engine finally started.

At Easter time, when we always holidayed, the autumn season and all it implied combined at high tide to make the waterways seem especially slow and serious. Sound travelled. We took the shortcut 'roads' marked with sticks and slipped between the oyster leases into Rileys Bay. Brimful and eerie. Cormorants sat on lease poles holding wings out to dry. At Rileys the bush came down to the water, mangroves in one corner and in the trees behind, bellbirds. A poor weatherboard house sat above a little sandy beach at which we kids often swam, having first negotiated the track past Shackleton's. Grazing on a small patch of open ground beside the house was a cow, which I believe to this day was deaf, although my brother Roger, a thoughtful man who is not by nature argumentative, disputes this fact. 'How could you know?' I just do. It occasionally bellowed, so it wasn't mute as well. Also in that corner, on those tide-muffled mornings, there would always be one crow calling out like an old woman complaining about a pain in her side.

Rileys was a nursery for fish. Ten cents for the first fish in the boat was a big incentive (decimal currency came in when I was six). Twenty cents for the first of edible size. Better fish sometimes came up out of the water: whiting, flounder, a bigger bream among the million babies.

The dads were patient, especially considering that in those days they hardly ever had us on their own. They untangled lines, helped get fish off hooks and dealt with snags, though we were taught to be self-sufficient. The many little bites kept us busy, but if I did get tired there were always fish to play with. I squeezed trumpeters to make them croak (gold-, brown- and silver-striped, you caught them drifting over weed), and in the bottom of the boat—in the gutter that held the bilge water—I gave swimming lessons to little bream, steering them up and down.

If it was windy we went instead to anchor in a bay back near our wharf—Purple Pumpernickel Bay we called it, after an ugly purple-painted steel yacht that was moored there. The water was deep there, dropping off close to shore. Its brooding emerald looked promising but it only ever delivered pesky babies.

In the afternoons, we seemed to be entirely free to go wherever we pleased, unsupervised. We racketed around the bush tracks or fished off the wharf while the dads took the boat out again for adult fishing time in a deep, deep spot which was hard to find (but when found was a piscatorial pot of gold); a secret place of mystery and many stories that was called . . . the Hole.

The Hole was situated quite nearby, and close to where the estuary narrowed. The greater part of the estuary filled and emptied through this neck, so the tidal forces were huge; indeed, the area was and is ominously known as the Rip.

The Hole, gouged out over millennia, could only be fished at the top or bottom of the tide, when the water slowed sufficiently that lines could reach the bottom and the big fish that lurked there could feed. Anything might come up from that extraordinary spot: red emperors, giant flathead, sharks—or nothing. Almighty tangles might ensue; the dads fished with cork handlines, and the swirling water was never completely still. Although what did we kids really know? We never went there.

While we waited for the dads to return we hung around the wharf. Sometimes we did take oysters, but not from leases, just ones on rocks in the shallows nearby, which we smashed open to use for bait when we ran out of prawns. We squeezed beads of pop-weed at each other; we tried to net mullet, those nervy vegetarians who would not take our hooks; we lay down on the old wharf timbers and hung our heads over the edge. I spent hours looking. At the mullet, the jellies, the sunlight ladders, the eddies. At toadfish going about their obsequious snooping.

When the putt-putt returned, the dads would sling us a wet sack if they'd had luck, and while they moored we ran on ahead with it to show the mothers. By then, with all jobs finally done, the women might be in the front room knitting. The front room was lined with beds around the walls—there was no lounge room. My bed was against the window, and in the mornings I woke before everyone else and looked out to early boats on the water, and to the houses and jetties on the opposite shore, which at that hour were gold-buttered.

The mothers did not seem to mind the wet sack on the floor, and we exclaimed together at what came out: the impressive ugliness of a dusky flathead; a snapper, its shining pink flanks glorious with aqua speckles. We always hoped for a jewfish, something to which Uncle Clive especially aspired but that I never saw him get. The sort of jewfish he plotted for would not fit in the sack.

At night, tucked in bed and daubed with calamine lotion, we listened to the parents having a few beers in the kitchen and playing cards; the cheerful noise of friends.

And then, not long after I turned eight, the news came that it was over.

•

I like to think I first went up to Woy Woy before I was born, when I was just a peanut-sized embryo in an ocean of my own. I don't know if that's true, and Mum and Dad are gone—Dad when I was 21—so I can't ask them now. But I don't see why that wouldn't have been so; I'm the youngest and my parents would have holidayed up there many times before having me. Out of all our visits, there are maybe half a dozen photos. In the earliest I'm about eighteen months old. There are ten of us in the boat, and I'm standing, leaning against my father's knee as he holds the tiller. (I remember now the way the tiller and rudder hooked on the back of the boat, the attaching mechanism so simple, a couple of metal spigots that dropped into collars. Why would I have observed such a thing so closely?) In that photo, it looks like we are going home.

Zero to eight. And then the big announcement. We were moving interstate.

It would be fun, we were told. An adventure. This time we would live only a short drive away from the water: Melbourne's Port Phillip Bay. We could go swimming often. We would get a boat of our own and we'd go fishing.

It did not take long for The Big Lie to be exposed. On the drive down to our new suburb on the Mornington Peninsula my parents made a poor choice in terms of public relations and took the back road, although in retrospect I suppose it didn't matter. The alternative, Beach Road, when I finally saw it, was not scenic by any standard I had known.

Through the car window the passing landscape was flat, flat, flat. Overcast skies, nondescript suburbs, light industrial; in open spaces the beige of wild oats. Flat, flat, flat.

This was it?

As a parental betrayal it was off the scale. Perhaps they had been replaced by aliens.

The Hole

My Woy Woy bush, the hills, the sandstone rocks, that old house, the green mysterious water. From all of that, I had been cruelly separated.

I was quiet. Maybe incapable of speech. They had me prisoner. Gazing out the car window I knew right then it would never get any better. There was only one thing to do: wait it out.

It would take years.

•

We did get a boat. I knew it was never going to be a putt-putt but thought for sure a tinnie. Dad bought the vessel from an elderly widow; it had been her husband's pride and joy—it was a great deal, apparently. Dad went to get it and backed it down our drive. It was bondwood. In its own way it was a beautiful thing, an open boat with graceful lines and varnished up to show off the golden grain of the ply; but bondwood? How could we ever get dirtily comfortable in such a craft, to do the industrious work of fishing? Bondwood. The choice was inexplicable. An alien boat for aliens.

And so, on the dull expanse of Port Phillip Bay—with its empty horizon and featureless shores, which even the tides seemed to have deserted, so indiscernible was their range—we launched the boat and ourselves. We caught flathead. Flathead and nothing else but flathead, little sand flathead, the only interest being whether we brought up one or two at a time on our two-hook rigs. And when they'd been in the bucket for a while they exuded slime. Pull one out and a curtain of gloop hung off it. To speed up the cleaning process back at home, Dad had to invent a rack so they could be de-slimed first with a blast of the hose.

·

Finally I grew up and, after detouring via Perth, was free at last to return to the Brisbane Water. A bridge had gone up across the Rip, but thanks to patches of national park the region hadn't changed too much. With increasing frequency I holidayed within sight of the old house, in a hamlet on the estuary from which the ocean could also be accessed. Double beauty.

Desperate to fish, I stalked the wharves and the beach to cast my rod, with haphazard results. I could not bear to fish beside other people and packed up the minute anyone came. The mere presence of even the quietest of strangers would keep me from the uninhibited level of concentration I needed if I was to get the fullest experience. The other sort of experience—just the doing, not the being—was, I thought, not worth having. In peak times this could be a major problem. I didn't have much money and I had nowhere to keep a boat on a trailer. It was frustrating. I could see Rileys Bay and all our old haunts.

Eventually, friends came to my rescue. The neighbour of one had a 10-foot fibreglass dinghy to give away. It was holed and the central third of the middle seat was missing, so a little restoration was required.

None of us had fibreglassed before, not even the blokes, and fibres of great length bristled from the fingertips of our washing-up gloves as we painted the sticky resin onto pieces of matting. The holes in the hull were quickly fixed and then the plan was to cut blocks of polystyrene foam to fit into the gap in the seat and glass the lot over. All good, except a chemical reaction took place and the resin melted the foam in seconds, eating it into shapes that were Gaudi-esque.

Next brainwave: raid the kitchen and cover the foam in aluminium foil.

It worked. When the fibreglass hardened, the blocks, like wrapped fruitcakes put aside to mature for Christmas, were visible trapped inside.

The boat was launched. It floated. I named it the *Squid*. It was ideal. Bashed and bomby, it could be left with impunity chained to a tree on the shore, waiting for me whenever I could return.

It turned out the *Squid* was a pig to row, and I soon got an outboard motor. But where to go? Well . . . Rileys, of course. I found a channel we hadn't used in my childhood and worked it on the drift into the bay, picking up the odd good thing and a regular feed of whiting. The only limitation on me now was the tide: to launch, to fish, to get back in, I had to have the right water. There was no cow in the corner at Rileys anymore but the bellbirds still tinked. Sometimes a sea eagle came out of the tall timber to make regal circuits. And in the very early morning, when everything was extremely still, fish jumped in front of the mangroves. Along with the familiar there was always something new to see. The green water slid on by.

•

I'd had the *Squid* for about eighteen months before my brother and his grown-up son came for a visit from Melbourne and took their first spin. The three of us had a great day drifting around Rileys together and we even caught a squid, which was a first. You never saw such an exquisite creature. The way its mantle flushed with iridescent dots of pink and turquoise.

The next day my nephew left to fly off somewhere, so Rog and I went out together. Here, at last, is where I get to the heart of my story.

There were hardly any bites. It happens sometimes. I don't know why. Days when even the entertaining babies aren't about, as if a master switch has been flicked to Off. We tried different lines of drift, different bait, anchored and put out lines for crabs—nothing.

12

By then there wasn't much left of the rising tide anyway; the few fish that were about would only become more inactive as the water slackened. So we picked up the anchor and for old times' sake set off on a tootle, steering through the same old oyster alley we used to travel. The trespass signs had gone from the leases over the years, though I can't think why the imperative to shoot should have lessened. Did oyster robbery go out of fashion as a crime?

We motored past our old wharf, looking up to where the house used to be; in the mid-1990s it was sold and demolished. And then, for fun, we anchored in Purple Pumpernickel Bay. I still fished there occasionally if the wind was up in Rileys, but despite the always-keen look of the water I'd never done any good. And it was the same for us that day. It didn't matter. We talked. I told Rog about the time I'd been there the summer before. I must be the only person in Australia, I said, who has had to move their boat to a new spot because it was surrounded by labradors. A pair of them had come charging down a private jetty and thrown themselves off the end at full pelt. Making a beeline for the *Squid*, they swam fast enough to create their own wakes, then settled in to circle insanely around the boat. Around and around they went, stupidly happy, and I worried they would tire or blunder into the lines I had out, wrapping them around their plunging paws. I don't know what they wanted but they did not return to shore until I motored away.

Still no bites. Well, nothing of any worth; a couple of tiddlers. What should we do? Stay or go home? And then Rog said quietly, wonderingly, as if it was a bizarre idea that at any moment might evaporate of its own accord, 'We could try . . . the Hole.'

Neither of us said anything. We sat there.

'We could,' I said finally.

But we didn't move. A strange and awful blankness was upon me.

'We're grown-ups now. We're allowed.'

'Yeah.'

In fact, we were middle-aged. Our parents were long dead. Uncle Clive was in decline and would soon be in a nursing home.

'It's the right time. It's just about the top of the tide.'

It was.

I said, 'Do you think we really could?'

But there was another consideration.

'Do you think you could find it?' asked Rog.

I didn't know. I had a marine chart on my bedroom wall at home and knew from it that the Hole was not a myth. It was 37 metres deep. But it was small, and I could only guess its position.

We started packing up. Got the motor going. We took it slowly, slipping between the boats moored around us and heading out towards the main channel and the Rip.

The Hole

As we approached I felt a growing apprehension. I studied the landfall on different sides to roughly judge the distance out. Throttled back. Looked around again. The surface of the water was calm, almost slicked, except for the delicate inscriptions that indicated eddies.

I stopped the engine.

Rog put the anchor over.

When I first got the boat I bought two anchors and two ropes, thinking I might use one from the bow and one from the stern when crabbing. I never did, but for some reason I put the two ropes together; I suppose I must have thought one day I'd come here.

The rope fed itself out over the side. We watched it dance across the gunwale in the automated fashion of a main thread on a knitting machine. Each of the ropes I had bought was 30 metres long. Down, down went the first. Down and down. And then it seemed to slow. But then the rope suddenly snaked and sped up and the stainless-steel clip that fastened the two ropes jerked into view, travelling up and over the bow: the second rope was away. We had found the Hole.

We were there.

Gradually we got used to it. Our lines took forever to get to the bottom and felt strange. But we started to relax.

It was true. We were not kids. We were allowed.

We didn't get any bites, but we began to enjoy our surroundings—that is, until about six other boats turned up and dropped their anchors right near us. Most of them were fancy plastic lumps with every sort of electronic gizmo hanging off—fish finders, GPS and so on. I was outraged. Here I was in a boat and still my fishing was spoilt by people coming too close.

I put on a last bait. It was nearly time to go. But we told ourselves our day had been successful anyway just by coming here. I left my rod unattended for a bit while I did some preliminary tidying, but when I picked it up again, oh my God, I had something heavy. Something big.

'Rog . . .'

Really big.

The rod bent. I pulled the big slow thing up and Rog got the net. It seesawed, it yawed, it took forever, but finally a dark shape materialised. Rog leant out and the shape nosed serenely into the net, though only its head seemed to fit; simultaneously Rog lifted and in a heavy, dripping arc in it came, landing thickly in the bottom of the boat. A huge flathead. Biggest one we'd ever seen—by a mile. Adrenaline pumping, we whooped and screamed.

'Suck eggs, you plastic heaps! Go the mighty *Squid*,' I hollered.

We were grown-ups.

•

I have fished the Hole many times since. My sister—bless her—
bought a wonderful holiday shack in the area, and being the
most feckless sibling and the only one resident in New South
Wales, I get to use it often. Finding the Hole straight off is not a
given, so when that second rope goes over I always feel a thrill.
And partially alarmed. Lots of times I come back with nothing.
But every now and then I scare the bejesus out of myself with
what I bring in: an octopus, small sharks and rays, a yellow
moray eel. Even a big flattie at the 80-centimetre mark can be
a heart-thumper to handle on your own. The thing is, you just
never know what will come up, because an infinite variety of
marine life swims in those waters. Sometimes, I must admit,
I'm not entirely sorry when a big thing gets away. It's never the
things I haven't caught that I regret; it's the things I didn't get
to see.

•

I have been privileged to share in the raising of a child, a boy
who is now a man of 25. In the wharf years, he got turned
off fishing—and who can blame him?—but more recently his
interest has rekindled. Alas, we only get to go out rarely. I put
him in charge of the boat, I try not to over-instruct, keep a lid
on my desire to impart the lore and love of the place as well as
the practical information he needs to be safe on the water.

Last Christmas Eve we fished the Hole together, and I caught a fish I thought I'd never catch: a jewfish. We yelled and hooted that day too. At three-quarters of a metre long, it was magnificent. An eyeful of silver. The mythic made material. I wished I could ring up Uncle Clive and tell him all about it, but he had died twelve months before.

I badly want to give my shared boy my own deep love of this place, because I know what comfort it can bring. To be steadied by that enduring core is to always be protected, but I know it can't just be bestowed. It must be lived.

I am a writer for whom words are usually scarce. I find them mesmerising: beautiful, strange, powerful things that take trouble to marshal. They tantalise, sometimes presenting themselves, sometimes retreating. Up they come in their own good time from the channels by the sandbanks, from the leases, from the Hole.

In my life I haven't been all that good at being around people. So when I'm dying it won't be the thought of leaving the world of people that will make me sad. It will be the thought of leaving my place. But I won't be frightened while I wait to go, I hope, because I will call up the watery paths of my childhood, of my life, and see *everything* in clearest detail. In my mind I'll walk the track past Shackleton's house down to Rileys, stopping at the ants' nest and pausing at the web of a St Andrew's Cross spider. I'll feel again the stippled texture of a pop-weed bead between my fingers; put my eye to a knothole in the floor of the old house. I'll sit in the *Squid* watching the slowing drag of the tide. That great volume of water, I always think, is like a cumbersome but magic wardrobe that must be dragged in and out of the same room several times a day according to a silent schedule.

Away it will slip, under me.

Dear shared boy, always remember that flash of silver in the deep. To live, even in the midst of love, is a lonesome business; but that quickening—the surprise of the marvellous glimpsed—keeps us going.

Things Seen

When Uncle Ev came back from the First World War there was something wrong with him. I don't think we kids were ever told quite what it was, but somehow we understood. It was shell shock, bad dreams, drink. But there was urgency to it. The kind of unspecified wrongness which Ev had brought back was terrible and dangerous, came close to taking his life.

Uncle Ev wasn't my uncle, he was Uncle Clive's uncle, so no family relation of mine, but Uncle Ev and I were connected by place. That's why, though the story of Uncle Ev was set two generations back in time, and about people I didn't know and would never meet, I paid attention.

It was Uncle Ev's father who came to the rescue. He quit his job and took his grown-up son away to camp in the bush at Rileys Bay on the Brisbane Water for however long it would take for him to get better. I don't know how he convinced him to go. Was subterfuge involved? Was it almost a kidnapping? Did Uncle Ev not care enough to refuse? The father left behind his wife and a comfortable home and the network of duties and ties that was his daily life: from all those roles and tasks he unhooked himself, in order to concentrate on one.

Why did the father bring him here, to this locale, particularly? Did someone suggest it, had the father been here before? I have no idea.

They probably travelled up by train to Woy Woy. But once arrived, they had to cross the estuary. The ferry service was regular in those days, calling in to isolated wharves on the bush side, as well as looping between patches of settlement on the populated western shore of the waterway. So while the father might have made do without a boat, to have one would have been better, a rowboat they could fish from and which they could pull up to the little beach at Rileys.

The hillside where they camped was steep—is steep—and thickly wooded, though dotted through with outcrops of rock. It folds around the bay, on windless winter afternoons throwing the shadow of itself far forward to turn the water glossy black, the jet of Edwardian mourning jewellery, liquid reflections precisely cut.

The wail of the distant train would have come over to them, piercing the quiet at timetabled intervals, but otherwise they lived with nature's sounds: abundant birds, the occasional splash of a fish.

I have no details of how it went, what form Ev's behaviour took, what the father did to assist his son when days or nights were bad. I imagine Ev filling his hands once more with tools that made sense: the handle of an axe; a pair of oars. Doing what hands are better off doing, as opposed to holding guns. That, I imagine, would help—the practice of simple chores. But that's the thing. I imagine. I do not know. How long did they stay? Six months, a year?

The story has only a few known truths. In that quiet and beautiful place, removed but still within sight of society across the water, Ev got better—or better enough to return to the city. A father's love and patience had saved his son.

The brevity and unadorned simplicity of the Uncle Ev story are its strengths. But because it's so short it's almost not a story. It's hard to situate. What reason is there to tell it outside a family gathering, or as a fleeting aside to a historical description of place? If the Ev story was a piece of music there would be silence at the beginning and end, giving it the extra space it needs to breathe to be its fullest self, time for the listener to sit with it a moment, and bring something of theirs to it.

Once, as a way of sharing the story, I might have tried to fictionalise it, plumping it up with drama, in the process destroying the spareness I admire.

•

Hidden at the back of the bookcase in the lounge room of our holiday house, behind volumes I judge to be of least interest to the strangers who sometimes rent the cottage, is a small notebook. To put it there is a risk. I put it there, in that semi-public place, not to invite the entries of others (as some casual finder might mistakenly think) but so it is handy, so I will remember to use it—I hope for many years. I wish I had started it earlier.

On the first page is the heading: *Things Seen*.

The notebook as first conceived was to be a list of living things seen in the area. It seemed likely that over time the diversity of the nature of this small place would prove to be quite remarkable. There would be pleasure when reviewing the evidence in the future.

I started off putting dates to entries because knowing the time of year a thing was once noticed might alert one to seeing it again. But I am mindful of a downside and the protocol may have to be modified. What if I am reading the notebook one day and realise that something delightful, once encountered

24

periodically, has not been spotted for years? Already I think of the hordes of soldier crabs that once occupied the mudflats near the church. It's more than likely I'll be an old lady holding the book with shaking, sun-cancered hands, turning page after page, crying.

Perhaps better not to put down years.

Only months.

I am careful when I add an entry not to be noticed by family members either, because I don't want to be self-conscious about what I write and I don't want to have to rebuff anyone's suggestions for inclusions, especially as any such suggestions would undoubtedly be made with much kindness and enthusiasm. Diversity is interesting, but it's not the whole point of the notebook. If it was the whole point, why would I mind the contribution of others? No. This is a list of things *I* have seen.

The importance of the book is as an aide-memoire. For each creature listed—on the page only a couple of words, little more than a noun or two—there's a detailed picture in my head. And not only that—attached to each mental image is the feeling of the experience I had of seeing.

So the list itself is bald:

The fairy penguin.
The dead sea snake at the beach.
The turtle swimming at the corner of the oyster lease.

But the notebook is a path to their re-creation. To renewed pleasure. To revisited wonder. To the intake of breath in that moment when my brain understood what my eyes were seeing.

For example: *The leatherjacket.*

Down at the extension wharf on a day when the water was preternaturally green and clear, I was watching the current and the graceful drag and sway of a long strand of sargassum weed attached to a piling when, by a small movement, the shape of a fish, a large leatherjacket, became discernible. It had been there all the time, feeding at the base of the weed, perfectly camouflaged in its patterned skin of antique lace, delicate fawns and browns.

As the water pushed the weed in dreamy pulses, the fins of the fish fluttered and trilled.

The leatherjacket.

•

If anyone understood the inerasable power of personal witness, it was Goya. He even put it into words. *Yo lo vi*, he wrote as the caption under the aquatint numbered Plate 44 in his 82-plate series, *The Disasters of War*, created during the Peninsular War, when the French invaded and occupied Spain between 1808 and 1814. 'I saw it.'

Scholars are careful to say the captions of the prints were 'probably' penned by the artist, but only because they are being strict with themselves. Only because they have no definitive proof. But there's really no need for such fussy legalese. Any writer looking at those illustrations and those words would tell you without hesitation that the same sensibility authored both—not for the way each caption suits its illustration, but for the way the plates and their captions work together, building sequentially into a narrative of despair. It's a narrative that contains complex internal rhythms; the lament of the captions is no monotone—it surges and pulls back, surges and pulls back, and the series as a whole is all the more devastating for this modulation.

Plate 44 is by no means the most disturbing. In many ways it's the least explicit. It depicts a stream of fleeing people. In the foreground are two startled men and a mother, carrying a baby, who tugs at the arm of a child falling behind. They are frozen in a moment of horror. Their hurried glances are to the right of frame, from where an unseen storm of violence is about to descend. It's clear the violence will overtake them. Will any survive? Looking at the illustration alone it's hard to judge. Perhaps, in the confusion of the chaos to come, some will escape. But then we must take the caption into account, and its plain, flat tone.

Yo lo vi.

I saw it.

It's a statement. A statement that leaves nowhere to go. The aftermath of the out-of-frame violence may be as unseen as the violence itself, but now it is surely not unknown. No one in the foreground will survive.

We must pay Goya's unembellished declaration the respect it is due.

'I saw it' can have the power of a red-hot brand.

What did Uncle Ev see?

•

Some art stares at death; some art seeks to ameliorate the fact of death by making death artful—a pretty dream concocted to distract us as the light switches off and we step into the ditch. To date, my custom has been to make art of the latter variety. It's white and middle class of me, a lucky girl brought up without strife in an affluent country in the second half of the twentieth century. The deaths I have seen have been isolated, the causes natural. But I want now, in my life and in my art, to look at everything more straight on. Not to duck from, or shirk, whatever is at hand. Probably ageing has caused this. The Romantic loses its appeal: the nub of a thing is what matters.

I think I am getting better at looking. My list has been good practice. Just by its existence it reminds me to stay watching for longer than might ordinarily be comfortable; to aim for a next level of noticing.

At first I wanted my list to be a pure thing; for it to have no other purpose than itself. I wanted to need nothing from it. But the items on my list are experiences and will not, I have discovered, stay locked away as isolated visions, as if in a museum. Unbidden, they are wont to put themselves to work to become part of something else.

My list, for instance, has offered up a way to extend the experience of Uncle Ev's story.

Given what we now know about neuroplasticity, it is more than possible that the brain might be retrained by feeding it with wholesome images to even up the balance of light and dark. Of course, only very intense, very concentrated images could do that. These new Things Seen must be just as inerasable, in their own way, as the old. Fresh witness is required, of almost equal power.

I suppose it's inevitable that over time the entries in my list of Things Seen have become slightly more expansive, especially where a circumstance is perhaps more noteworthy than the creature it features. For example:

The raven that comes down out of the banksias to the sand at the quiet end of the beach. Picks at the wrack.

Sometimes the creature of the entry is absent:

The boat and underwater feet.

In the days before I saw that, I had been thinking about Ev.

I was setting off to go fishing. The water is very shallow where I keep my boat. I wait for the tide to come in over the flats, a silty mixture of sand and mud. The dinghy is flat-bottomed and floats in only a few centimetres of water, but I must wade out a long way—to nearly thigh level—before I can put the motor down and jump in. Sometimes, when I am early on the tide, I feel like I could walk the whole way to my fishing spot.

I trekked this day in shin-deep water, very clear. The sand was lunar, pocked all over with small crab holes, and I was watching my feet so as not to step on one of the dinner-plate-sized stingrays which often lie there. I was absorbed, concentrating on the footprints I was making. And then I came across the unexpected line of yesterday's footsteps leading out. I was surprised. The tidal movement of the past 24 hours had made them sloughed at the edges and clumsy, but they were not erased, as I would have presumed. Abominable snowman tracks, in a straight line, but stumbling. Effortful. For Ev, taking his boat out at Rileys Bay and seeing the same, they might have been a reminder of muddy steps on battlefields.

I held the boat beside me, gentled it along. I walked my new footsteps beside the old, head down, the shallow moonscape

30

and the yeti steps my whole field of view. In this hyper-focused state I walked the crystal water. Thought-less. And then, in turn, this picture plane was suddenly interrupted, this time by the intersecting tracks of a large bird. The three stick lines of each foot were so fine and sharply etched, so seemingly fresh, that at first I couldn't understand how they could be laid underwater. I laughed, in a kind of delighted shock. They crossed my old prints on a determined diagonal. They were going somewhere too. They were alive.

It was the kind of new memory capable of turning some other dark one back to the wall.

And then, a metre away, a ray I hadn't seen shot off.

My Life and the Frame

I.

I used to be a television camera operator. The only thing I ever liked about it was the frame.

Don't get me wrong: I wanted to be a television camera operator. I trained for it, and it was my first proper job, but I wasn't interested in any of the technical stuff I had to master. I only liked it because I was putting a frame around things. What I liked was selection and composition, I suppose, especially when I worked on outside broadcasts. The tension and excitement of wielding my frame, this halo of attention, for as long as I possibly could until the subject moved beyond where I could follow—thereby destroying the picture I was making—was thrilling. It involved a deep level of concentration, of unthinking (the same sort from which the best writing comes), and letting the body be, to do what it needs to do, what it knows to do, without instruction.

Let me explain with an example. I'm at the football. I'm about 23 years of age. I've been allocated the ground camera for the season. Every week, at whatever ground we happen to be, my spot is right on the fence line at the midway point on the belly of the oval, equidistant from the goals. I'm working for the ABC in Perth and we're covering the local Aussie Rules league, which in those days, with a national competition still years away, was closely followed.

To cover the game we use four cameras. Two cameras are positioned side by side way up in the grandstand: the wide-shot camera, which provides the go-to safety shot keeping all the main action in view; and the close-up camera, with its formidable snout of a lens. The close-up camera is operated by old Ray, who has a special genius for this task alone. He's revered for it, but on other types of broadcasts is relegated to a do-nothing camera where his lack of interest in any other aesthetic or finesse can do no harm. On the close-up camera, Ray can hold a tight shot of a far distant kicker, then whip-pan unerringly to the catcher before the ball arrives, somehow divining not just the intended destination, but the actual. To appreciate the skill in this, you have to understand that during the pan the viewfinder is no assistance: at that speed, on that lens, all vision is blurred.

The third camera is mine, used to take the viewer down to ground level and in among the action. The fourth is the boundary camera, a portable affair, handheld, though still cabled back to the van. The boundary camera is rarely in the right place at the right time, so the drama it is capable of catching is only sporadically added to the coverage, but it's also handy for the less glamorous jobs of showing players coming on and off the field and post-match interviews.

Hours before the game begins, our trucks pull up, disgorging boxes of equipment. Many trips are required to cart gear to each of the places it needs to go. Two people to a lens box, two to the body of the camera, two to the accessories box, two to lug the canvas bag which holds the head of the tripod, one seriously fit fellow to shoulder the tripod itself.

There is something satisfying about the communal, repetitive task of carrying the equipment. There is not much thought involved; one thing patiently brought then the next, backwards and forwards. Then there is the job of putting the camera together in its big building blocks. As we work, the Colt and Reserve grade games are played, and spectators drift into the stands—the nutters and the diehards first.

Along with the increase in surrounding activity comes a rising level of tension in me, barely discernible at first, but ratcheting up whenever play in the early games comes close to my position. The sound of the smack of body on body is particular and confronting. It goes unheard in the main game, where the general hullabaloo masks the impact of collisions. The Colts players rarely call out or make much other noise themselves beyond the odd grunt of effort, so, like mime actors in a dumb show who suddenly come together and clap hands, the slap of bodies is startling, seems somehow against the laws of the game. In that sound, the animal work of sport is exposed.

With my camera set up and tests and practice over, I lean against the scaffold railing of my low camera platform, waiting for the game to begin. How will I go? I don't indulge my nerves but let them buzz in the background. There is nothing to be done now that can affect the fate of the day. My job, after all, is to react.

Finally the siren sounds, the whistle blows, the first ball is bounced: the time has arrived for me to work with my travelling frame.

Come into my viewfinder. See what a glorious thing it is to move with this young man as he runs, swooping with him as he scoops the ball one-handed from the ground. (In the dark corner of my viewfinder the red light pings on. We're on air.) He spins out of a tackle, bounces the ball, accelerates and bounces again. He's travelling left to right; we give him running room, or looking room as it's called in the trade, keeping him back near the left-hand edge so he's got open space ahead, otherwise he'll seem in danger of banging up against the wall of the right-hand edge, the frame suddenly turned into a prison cell.

He sprints, every muscle straining, glances over his shoulder to check on unseen pursuers gaining; we're keeping up, I'm keeping up, in all my movements fluid, pulling focus while panning, zooming. In one ear of my headset the van people are talking, commentators blurt into the other, but I'm hearing nothing, I'm in the beautiful blank zone of the picture for as long as it keeps going. Don't think, don't think, as soon as I think I'll throw focus forward instead of back and all that swift joy will dissolve into shameful blur; the worst of it will be the rock back and forth, the panic to find sharpness again, *Which way?*, the indecision. Don't think, stay in the blank, it can't last forever, it's already been too good for too long.

He veers, the chasing pack steers him towards us. The red light's still steady. I won't be able to hold him, or them. *Get off my shot*, I want to yell to the van, *I can't hold them.*

With a tumble of bodies the frame overfills (somewhere in there my boy must be smashed), they explode towards me, it's going, it's going . . . The red light blinks out. It goes. In a million tiny pieces of action that cannot be contained, the composition in my frame flies apart.

I swing my lens to begin again, hunt down a new shot. Next time, if it's not the movement of the players that wrecks my composition, it will be the ball. More than once in a game, its erratic bounce makes fools of us all.

•

At half-time the van gets us to look for shots to cover the commentators' chat, or as background for the scores or stats. I like this too. Now I have the chance to go off looking on my own. The camera is my dancing partner, though it's anchored to the spot. I take it by its two arms and sweep it around. I rove and select. It has started to rain. A close-up profile of a man in the crowd, a transparent drip forming on the rim of his cap and falling; pull focus to the rabbity-faced boy beside.

Sometimes the frame puts a little dignity around something that ordinarily manages without.

I offer up a shot of fence pickets curving pleasingly away. It's ignored. A seagull next to a puddle. They take that. Rain pincushions the surface of the water. The snowy white breast of the bird. So pure it's taking me over. I could fall right into that patch of white and live there for a while. Intensifications of vision like this are not uncommon for me, probably because my viewfinder makes for tunnel vision. And the picture is black and white, so to my eye something like the red beak of the bird is only a darker grey contrast, not the bright modifier it would be to the people at home watching in colour.

The rest of the game will be hard. With the arrival of the rain there's a drop in light and the depth of field is drastically reduced, meaning nothing will stay in focus long. Tweaking will be constant. I have no choice but to trust the unseen wire between my eye and my right hand. Let my body do its best. Whatever picture my frame finds to make won't be long possessed.

•

In those moments, moment by moment, so long ago, what was it I really framed? Perhaps it was endeavour.

II.

For some years now I have been writing an Australian colonial baroque novel. *Oh really?* I hear you say with a false note of cheer. Unsaid, but loud and clear, are the follow-up comments: *How the heck do those two things go together?* And: *How will you pull it off?*

I didn't go looking for the baroque in my story. A little element of it jumped into my imagination and then, inevitably, more pushed and shoved to come in. Because that's just how the baroque is. It became my unshakeable, indispensable, difficult friend: the sort that takes over a party, is hilarious, then wrecks it, but without whom the party wasn't worth going to anyway.

The hangover came later, but in the first flush of acquaintance I wanted to find out all I could about the period.

I started by refamiliarising myself with much that was half remembered from high school art history classes, commencing with the Council of Trent (1545–63). This was the rather long meeting of Catholic clerics dedicated to reinvigorating the Church to meet the threat of Protestantism. Spreading out of the north, Protestantism, with its insistence on personal responsibility and pointed preference for plainness and economy, offered an alternative to the overbearing authority of Catholicism.

As part of its counterattack, the Council of Trent commanded Catholic artists to enthral the commonfolk: to win, for keeps, their hearts and minds through art, using whatever dramatic or emotional means necessary. Go big, go grand, they said. Turn our weaknesses into strengths. Make visible the glory of God. Make beautiful the power of the Church.

And so began the baroque period of art production, which lasted from around 1600, with the emergence of Caravaggio and friends, through to its late or rococo phase in the mid-1700s.

As I studied the preoccupations and stylistic characteristics of the period and the great practitioners, my heart rate quickened. Across the centuries, just as the old priests at Trent intended, I felt charged.

Who could resist the baroque's V8 throb, its largesse and exuberance, its struggle with light and dark? Its willingness to slum it while depicting the divine? Its love of risk? (Think of Bernini's sculptures, some so twisted and buffeted by the forces of nature and God, the artwork itself seems bound to crack. *Put that hammer and chisel down, Bernini; not one more tap!*)

So much about the baroque is modern: the mixing of media to achieve maximum effect; its kinetic desire; its interactivity—the way it sometimes bursts out of the frame to claim attention, pouring itself forth, playing also with the idea of witnesses, viewers, participants, peeking in and climbing out. With its widespread use of trompe l'oeil, the baroque seeks to extend reality, and perhaps ecstatically warp it, too.

My baroque homework drew me on through the period until, eventually, I was led to Tiepolo. In particular, to the Würzburg Residence in Bavaria and the ceiling fresco he painted there, above a stone staircase so big it occupies a hall of its own.

Perhaps this sounds like I visited in person. I did not. I first encountered the place on TV, then via unsatisfactory pictures on the internet (too small), then, for a while, via quite a good book I borrowed from the library—although a few vital plates were missing, cut out by an image-greedy previous borrower.

In Tiepolo, in Würzburg—in the biggest fresco in the world—I finally found validation for my novel.

•

The Würzburg fresco was painted by Giovanni Battista Tiepolo in 1750–53. Already recognised as the master painter and decorator of his age, the artist was summoned from Venice for the commission. Civilisation and colonisation are the subjects of the work. Called *Allegory of the Planets and Continents*, the central part of the ceiling depicts the overseeing activities of the classical gods in heaven, around which the four continents are arrayed: Europe, Asia, Africa, America. The fresco is dynamic with the turmoil of change. Allegorical and mythic figures mix with the strange and sometimes fantastical creatures of each land; indigenous cultures and economies clash with the invading.

My amateur art education is so hit and miss I didn't realise this was a common topic of the day, though I should have twigged. It was the Age of Discovery and art everywhere made a point of showing off new goods and pillaged riches, while also confirming the fitness of Europe to rule and take the lot. In return, the so-called primitive continents got some of the trappings of Western civilisation, and the Word of God; not a bargain they had much say in.

The date of Tiepolo's Würzburg work rocked me. Just seventeen years after he put down his brush, Captain James Cook sighted the coast of Australia. What would Tiepolo have painted to represent the fifth continent had he known of its existence?

Suddenly it didn't seem so far-fetched for me to think, as I had, of the newly seen land of Australia as somehow being itself baroque, a misshapen pearl, a last treasure—a place where pre-Enlightenment forces, both Indigenous and European, could still be active. In short, I wanted to blow up all those old, passive depictions of Sydney Cove, and the baroque seemed the way to do it.

The fresco was a vindication of everything I'd been leaning towards, even if the logic of how it would work in my novel still lay just out of reach. In a state of possibly unstable joy, I pored over my Tiepolo book.

The fresco is marvellous in every regard. The depictions of the continents run frieze-like above each of the four walls and the viewer 'travels' to them, physically visiting each continent as she ascends the stairs and looks up, turning to 'discover' a new vista at each landing. Tilting her head back to take in the central part of the ceiling, the visitor sees the gods in the clouds, and right up their gowns. There, Tiepolo's lightness of touch and genius for airiness reigns.

In the political dramas arrayed around the staircase, Tiepolo shows a pragmatic understanding of human behaviour and driving motivations. Complex compositional lines create the sense of many movements happening at once. Here and there the action threatens to spill out of the frame—then actually does, with people, animals and material goods toppling over a trompe l'oeil parapet, which functions as the fresco's bottom edge. Some figures, having fallen out of the picture, are seen desperately trying to climb back in, scrambling to grab or defend what's theirs before it's carried off by someone else. But the illusion is taken a step further. In each corner of the stairwell there is a real cornice of decorative plasterwork where sculptures of naked youths perch on a ledge that looks the same as the painted parapet. Several of these statues convincingly appear to have one leg in the painting and one leg out, as if they had swivelled on their seat, straddling it to get a better look at all the commotion going on behind. In one corner the youths' legs are grey, as if in the shadow of the dark cloud which looms in that quarter of heaven. In this way, even the weather comes out into the room.

The blurring of the edge between realms is complete and the painted world is so thoroughly activated it cannot be enclosed. Untidy, barbaric, joyous, it pours out into the thoroughfare of the staircase, a transit place of real people and real movement.

This is Art wanting to meet Life.
And to me, it was riveting.

•

But why?

Why did I find this idea of frame-breaking so arresting? My TV days were so long in the past I'd forgotten my former relationship with the frame, but now they came back to mind. I began to see that it was really my own, old history that caused the research to speak to me, because I also remembered something else.

Long before Tiepolo, well before the viewfinder, there was the window.

III.

The window was really a series of windows running along the whole front of the house. And the house was the old Woy Woy holiday cottage our family went to with friends when I was a kid.

The house had only two bedrooms, and the front room, which had the feel of a closed-in verandah, was the main one. Single beds were arranged end to end around the walls; against one of the short walls my parents had a double. My bed was under the window.

Every day I woke before anyone else and my first thought was for the window. Though the main elements of the view did not change, every day, sitting up, I was eager to see how it looked: weather, light, boats wrought endless variations to arrangements.

The house was perched on a bushy hill, so the view was layered. Trees in the lower foreground; in the middle distance the blue strip of estuary; on top of that the opposite shore with its fussy detail; beyond that, ocean, Lion Island, more hills—sky.

Morning light in morning air. Everything gold-edged, intense.

Through that first frame I looked—I studied—for a little while alone, but in the sleep-muffled company of people I loved.

Next to my bed was a traymobile where Uncle Clive would put the tea things when he woke, but a lower shelf of that vehicle was the keeping place of something very wonderful. A pair of binoculars. They were small and made of brass, very old, perhaps once used more often at the opera than on the seven seas. Perfect for a child. In my first novel, I gave my childhood experience of looking through them to the adult female protagonist. At her dad's house, she idly picks up his binoculars and scans the bay, bumping over the water until she isolates a putt-putt motorboat. She moves with it, giving it a little bit of open water to cut into. What she's got before her eyes is an old-fashioned motion picture, grainy and unsophisticated and containing one simple uncluttered truth. It's just a picture of a boat moving through water, and, to her, it's lovely.

That's exactly what I saw, that's exactly what I thought, as a kid. And I suppose it's why I later loved my viewfinder.

The images of childhood are mythic, steering thought and lives in ways not always easy to discern. Here I was, only just beginning to understand how a humble window helped shape mine.

IV.

Frames began as protective edges around paintings and were 'engaged'; that is, physically attached and inseparable from the artwork. Any ornamentation of the frame was thus a permanent part of the experience of viewing.

By the Middle Ages, some paintings used as altarpieces were literally 'housed' in frames designed to look like church architecture. These frames paid reverence to the sacred images they contained, and protected them as treasures. The paintings *were* valuable treasures, made of gold leaf and pigments ground from rare and expensive minerals.

During the Renaissance, illusory effects involving the frame first emerged. Painters began to incorporate elements of the frame into their pictures, softening the transition between the real and the painted. Effects were also tried where objects such as books or knives seemed to protrude out of the picture plane.

Canvas slowly replaced wooden panels as a painting surface, and the frame became an accessory and 'disengaged', or separate to the painting. As the individual skill of particular artists became more celebrated, craftsmen took over the job of framing. They, in turn, began to assert themselves, especially in Italy during the baroque period, with frames becoming more and more elaborate. Intricately carved and gilded, these frames proclaimed the trophy status of the paintings, and, by featuring crests and emblems, drew attention to their proud owners. In northern Europe, as one might expect, the fashion remained more restrained.

Gradually Paris took over as the centre of frame making, turning the eighteenth and nineteenth centuries into a golden age for the craft.

In the nineteenth century, advances in printing meant images were far more widely available. To use them as decor was finally within the reach of many. Prints required frames— so frame making became an industry, not much connected with artists. When artists did take back control, they reacted against extravagant designs. The impressionists and post-impressionists opted for plain frames painted in neutral colours to complement works, although few of those frames have survived. Collectors mostly replaced them, choosing frames which spoke to the status and value of the pictures, or which matched collection styles.

In the twentieth and twenty-first centuries, it's obvious that artists have used frames when and however they pleased. Now when museums and private collectors need to reframe works, they select frames which best serve the intentions of the piece. But the ethos, reputation and architectural setting of a gallery or collection also 'frames' works in various ways. I can't help but think here of the area where Sidney Nolan's Ned Kelly paintings are hung in the National Gallery of Australia. It's a specially designed, separate room, which not only announces and frames the Kelly series, but its oblong proportions, and the physical experience of being in it, replicates what it might be like to look through the slot of the bushranger's iron mask. In the paintings, Nolan is playing all the time with the mask's eye-slot and using it as a frame.

A weird fact about the frame is that empty frames demand pictures: so much so that an empty frame will convert whatever can be seen within into a picture—even a blank wall. In the often-empty Kelly eye-slot you can see something of what might be called the great loneliness of the frame: it's always in search of something.

The Kelly/Nolan room at the NGA is an echo chamber of frames, of presentation and re-presentation.

Because that's what frames do. They act to cordon off reality, pushing away distraction to signal an aesthetic work, and draw attention in. This subject, they say, is worthy of our further consideration. The academic Karsten Harries puts it nicely, in a way that reminds me of my viewfinder days: frames help us attend to 'the silent speech of things'.

Something else Harries says interested me very much. During the late baroque, the frame began to collapse as a border, on occasion invading the picture to the point of becoming part of it, and vice versa. (We see this with Tiepolo at Würzburg.) But then there's a further phase where the frame goes completely wild and neurotic. Some of the most extreme examples are seen in drawings and etchings where picture elements, such as trees, 'grow' outwards, morphing to become an intricate drawn frame within an actual frame. Furthermore, these secondary, drawn frames often fail to contain their central image, resulting in a kind of bizarre feedback loop. With all the picture elements battling for supremacy, the status of the central image is undermined. Harries suggests this indicates a repressed anxiety about the approach of modernism. The decay of the frame raises the question: What is Art?

•

In the basement library of the Art Gallery of New South Wales, where I investigated the frame, I wrote up my notes. While I was typing out quotes from academic theory to do with the frame, the words in common use struck me: *imprisoning/ freedom, subordination, transgression, authority, containment, contamination, protective, restrictive.*

They were words anyone might read in a book about a penal colony.

Then I thought of Aboriginal rock art and rock galleries and couldn't recall ever seeing a line drawn around an image to isolate it or privilege it over another. In the Indigenous world, it would seem, art was never separate from life.

Among our other tyrannies, we whities brought the frame.

V.

Writing a novel, as you can see, sometimes takes its author off in unexpected directions. *Yes*, I hear you reply impatiently, *but did all this baroque/frame research pay off?*

It did not.

I spent four years. I had two good characters; some good, unexpected ideas went unexpectedly well together; I had chunks of good writing. But whatever I tried, I couldn't get the novel to breathe by itself, to start making its own action.

In a last hope that undivided attention would make the difference, I ditched my only reliable income stream and quit my part-time job.

Still the novel refused to be. And there was no denying it: though the good bits were good, the worst were fake.

I wondered if the baroque was to blame after all. Was the baroque all gesture?

Critics of the period say for all the wealth and potency of its images, it leaves the viewer feeling empty. Its vibrancy is superficial, its noise merely noise. The harshest critic even said that, at its core, it's frigid.

That bothered me.

I put the novel aside but continued to think about those negative assessments.

After returning again and again to my favourite baroque artworks, I've come to the conclusion that I don't agree. There's too much relish and appreciation for life in the baroque for the frigid and empty charges to stand. No, something else is the matter with the baroque. At the heart of the baroque is frustration. The baroque puts its arms out and complains—*I give you so much, this power, this beauty, this force poured forth, and yet it's not enough. It's everything I have, but it's not enough.* Because there's something pure at the heart of art that can't be wholly communicated. We glimpse it, we manage to show it in parts, but it remains itself, unattainable and intact. The baroque weeps with frustration at this. It wants to pull that thing out by the roots and thrust it into your hands. But it can't be done. This is really the message the baroque has for the rest of Art.

It can't be done.

But, dear baroque, your temperament is to die trying.

VI.

The novel had failed. Perhaps not permanently, because there was still a maddening pulse at its centre, but certainly for the time being—maybe for a very long time. My material was exhausted, I was exhausted. I needed to take stock. I needed to repair.

I decided to go fallow.

The more I thought about it the more I warmed to the idea: I would go dormant but in a way that was still active. If I opened myself up and calmly listened, there might be all sorts of things to hear—things I didn't immediately have to turn into something else, as writers often feel compelled to do. In fact, I would be anti-production. I would read and walk and look at art and people and nature, and I would let whatever came my way wash over me and through me, and then let it go. I felt tired and sad and strangely like I wanted to find some missing level of maturity, but I also had a half-formed notion that if I took that mood to the experience of fallowness and went carefully and slowly ahead, it might be possible for this period to become a kind of artwork in itself. Perhaps that sounds hippie-ish; but it could be more, a lot more, than a desolate dribbling away of time.

My chief pleasure during the fallow was to read visual artists talking about their work and ways of seeing. The difference but adjacency in their thinking freshened my own. David Hockney became my favourite. I like the way he lives a life of inquiry, arranging every aspect of daily living around his investigations. When intrigued by something he's noticed, or when moved to interrogate an accepted orthodoxy, Hockney undertakes elaborate, semi-scientific experiments. The artworks that *might* result are not an end in themselves but part of his ongoing engagement with visual perception.

In a book by Martin Gayford called *A Bigger Message: Conversations with David Hockney*, Hockney has some interesting things to say about the frame. Because he's so fascinated by the way the eye moves around a picture to read it, he's also very interested in edges. He talks about Jacques Tati's 1953 film *Monsieur Hulot's Holiday*, in which one scene is set at a large railway station with multiple platforms. The comedy relies on a static frame. A group of people find themselves on the wrong platform. As trains arrive and depart the people rush downstairs to pop up on another platform, also the wrong one. And so it goes on. The comic tension arises out of the confusion, but also because of the way Tati uses space. The trains come and go from the frame horizontally, while the people travel up and down vertically. In the unseen underground tunnel that connects the platforms, they also notionally travel *below* the frame.

Hockney says really good filmmakers and photographers like Tati understand the screen and know how to get the best out of it. He notes that big effects don't necessarily create a more immersive experience.

When he found himself unimpressed with 3D cinema, he realised it was because the 3D camera, with its fixed position, was unable to interpret the world in the same way as the human eye, which constantly samples from here and there as it scans a scene. To see if he could do better, he ran an experiment, mounting nine high-definition cameras on a car, which was driven down an avenue of gloriously blossoming hawthorn. The results were projected onto a nine-way split screen. He was pleased with the way it opened up new modes of narration. Essentially, he and his assistants had made a very fluid lens. They'd succeeded in making a flat picture that allowed the eye to look the way it likes to look in real life—roving and taking in multiple things in a split second.

When I watched the hawthorn video online, I found it unexpectedly involving. It was surprisingly beautiful, for starters, but I was drawn in to it—became almost latched on to it—because it really did command the physical engagement of my eye. I *entered* the picture, moving past the psychological fence of the frame.

Still ruminating on the frame, Hockney talks about a visit to the Metropolitan Museum in New York, where he was invited to look at a Chinese scroll. About 30 metres of it was unwound on the floor and Hockney shuffled along on his knees looking at it for hours. The scroll dated from 1770 and depicted an emperor passing through a city which was represented in its entirety, along with its population of thousands of individualised figures going about their business.

That same day, museum staff asked if he'd like to see something else. Downstairs they had a panorama of Versailles, painted by John Vanderlyn in 1818–19. To view it, Hockney he had to stand on a platform in the centre of the circular panorama. He immediately understood the contrast the staff wanted to show him. 'We're stuck in a fixed point [where the city doesn't change]. But in the Chinese scroll we've just been travelling through a great city.'

In Vanderlyn's day not many people in the Western art world knew about such scrolls, because they're impossible to reproduce in books, and to be correctly viewed they should be unwound in person.

You don't entirely unravel a scroll; you turn it continually. So it doesn't really have edges on the sides. The bottom edge is you, and the top edge is the sky . . . [We] found out that the Chinese had rejected the idea of the vanishing point in the eleventh century because it meant that you— the viewer—weren't there. You weren't moving. If you're not moving, in a way you're dead.

In the next breath Tiepolo's ceiling over the grand staircase in Würzburg is mentioned. This, Hockney says, is an example in Western art where, as the spectator moves, more of the painting is revealed.

Amazing, actually that staircase is just fantastic. The colour is wonderful. It's one of the outstanding things of the eight-eenth century . . . Imagine what fabulous theatre it would have been to stand here in the eighteenth century, with all the people coming up and down that grand staircase, all the flunkies at the side. Looking at the ceiling, looking at them. It would have been incredibly splendid . . . The drawing is astonishingly ingenious.

57

The Chinese scroll, the Versailles panorama, Tiepolo's staircase . . .

The Versailles panorama!

Suddenly I remembered my long-forgotten high school art project.

VII.

I was always hopeless at art—the actual doing of it as opposed to the art history component—but something made me persist with the subject right through to my final year. I chose photography as a way of getting around my lack of any other practical skill, but I wasn't even particularly good at that. Technically, photography was all a bit fussy for me; and I didn't really know what to take pictures of. Macro lens shots of flowers or fern leaves—yawn. But then I had an idea. How it came to me I no longer recall, but my idea was to empty out a small, almost square room in the school's oldest building and photograph it. The room was then a storeroom, but years ago had been a boarder's bedroom. It was upstairs. It had one window, which overlooked a courtyard. A dark wooden picture rail ran around the walls, which were painted white but were bashed about. I decided I would stand in the middle of the room taking multiple pictures until I had turned 360 degrees and captured the four walls, floor to ceiling, in overlapping frames. Then I would build a circular structure, a bit like a massive lamp-shade. The lampshade would be about 3 metres in diameter, its walls a metre and a half high. I would mount the photos inside the structure, thus reconstructing the room, only now, physically, the room would be circular. The structure would have to be suspended somehow and the viewer would need to duck under to enter. Once inside, the viewer would stand in the middle and turn, just as I had when taking the pictures. Just as David Hockney had when viewing the Versailles panorama.

This was 1978. I was a schoolgirl. In those days no one got involved with kids' projects—not the parents, not the teachers—so I didn't expect any help. But neither did I have a clue how to build my big lampshade. I didn't know how it could be suspended (it would be heavy), or how to make it transport-able. I wasn't even sure if the photos could be coherently joined together. And I had no money.

What did others think of my big idea? I don't remember outright scorn, just indifference, as if it wasn't worth the bother of thinking about because it was already obvious I wouldn't be able to pull it off. Nobody asked what it might mean, which was just as well because I didn't know that either, although it was never a matter of just being clever—fitting a square space into a round hole. There was something about the original room that was important. It had an atmosphere of austere weariness that was not unpleasant; that invited stillness. In order to see all the stillness of the reconstructed room, the viewer had to move inside the lampshade, and that paradox, between stillness and movement, was probably key. The cell-like nature of the space, in a monastic sense, was surely in play too; this was a place of refuge and restrictions—which is psychologically interesting given it was once a boarder's bedroom, and that I was waiting to leave school and go out into the world. But that's all hindsight talking. All I knew at the time was that my idea made me feel buoyant. It's a feeling I would recognise now as a pretty good indicator I'm on to something worth pursuing.

I tried to think of structural designs and lightweight materials for construction, but the scale of the thing, the logistics, the mathematics of it all defeated me. All I succeeded in doing was wasting a good deal of time. There was nothing for it; I had to give up. But what would I do instead? A lethargy settled on me. No other ideas appealed. For months I procrastinated. The deadline for submission approached.

Eventually I took a few urban grunge photos to go with one I'd taken of a supermarket, the side wall of which had been graffitied with the words *White Machine*. On the weekend before the Monday deadline I stuck the photos onto pieces of cardboard and tried to hang them from a mobile made out of coathangers.

As soon as I began the task, a cavern opened up in the bottom of my stomach. I already knew my artwork wasn't going to be much good, but I'd been so uninterested in it for so long, I wasn't prepared for the fact that in truth it was abominable.

I panicked.

I had trouble stopping the strings from sliding on the hangers; the weight distribution was impossible to organise; strings broke; hangers tipped. Strings pulled out of photos. It was all so tin-pot, so homemade, so flimsy. I would never get everything attached and balanced, and even if I did, my humiliation would not be over. In the cold light of the last day there was no getting around it: the photos were poor, the whole thing was rubbish. I deserved to fail. And the worst thing of all—it was my own fault. I might never have been capable of creating art, but I could have avoided this last-minute debacle.

Surrounded by cotton reels, coathangers and cardboard, I wept.

In the end, my brother could no longer bear my distress. Home for the weekend from teachers' college, he stepped in to help. Somehow, piece by piece, the hanging contraption was cobbled together then carefully folded into a cardboard box for transportation.

In the car on the way to school the next day, I could not bear to look at the box on the seat beside me. My stupid

White Machine. How the examiners would keep it in one piece as they lifted it out, I did not know. I did not care. All I wanted was never to see it again. And I had my wish.

I must have blitzed the art history exam, because somehow I managed to scrape through the subject overall, though I could never think of the experience again without cringing. In fact, I did my best to suppress every memory of it. Forgotten, too, was the artwork behind it; the one that never was. Because I was ashamed of that as well—my big idea—the hubris of it, the overreach. The pointless dreaming.

But the Versailles panorama prompted me to recall my thwarted seventeen-year-old self and feel kinder towards her. Thanks to the baroque and going fallow, I now know that the pleasure of thinking a big idea is not to be dismissed as nothing. Even if the idea is never realised, the thinking is real, and enlarging and sustaining; as much a part of art and the life of inquiry as actual production. But most importantly, thanks to Tiepolo, I finally understand the impulse behind my grand folly. My lampshade. My circular room.

While I was attending to the silent speech of the original room and re-presenting the experience of being in it all those years ago, I was also, surely, trying to step inside the frame.

Life wanted to meet Art.

Up in my coastal holiday place I have experienced this.

VIII.

Several times in recent years I've seen windless days up the coast that are in every way so perfect, I have stood beside the bay and wished I could cram it all into my mouth. The glass of the water, floury blue body of sky, the scents in the air, the boats, the shore-edge trees: the very *poise* of all things.

Days like these only occur in autumn or spring. My encounters with them begin with the normal enough wish to breathe them in, but as the day goes on and I stop what I'm doing to look and look again, the impulse grows to throw my hands out wide to somehow grab the day and drag it to my lips.

When a spring bushfire burnt out the coastal ridge that protects the inlet from the sea, I went up to survey the aftermath. The obliterated heath was shocking, but also grimly beautiful: only black sticks were left, standing like abandoned spears in acres of ash. How strange it was, to see the Pacific Ocean carrying on with its usual blue business beyond this newly stricken foreground.

On either side of the gravel road on which I walked, still-warm powdery drifts of ash looked like beds to be lain down upon. I wished I could. I would sink into that softness, letting the ash cover me so that when I rose I would be coated in the finest dust, wearing it as I walked.

Leaving the ridgeline at a fork in the track, I veered away from the sea to travel on the inlet side of the hill through a small angophora forest, also burnt. The trees, which in normal health were goitred and twisted, still stood, but now were charcoal. Many had been hollowed out. Some trunks were split open at their base like blackened skirts. I could see how flames must have poured and roared through inner tunnels to triumph from the throats of trunks and from the ends of amputated branches, as if the fire was dressing itself in the fluid shape of the tree, thrusting arms of flame through sleeves. Everywhere stood these empty black evening gowns, each one sophisticated and original. Why hadn't some haute couture designer made dresses modelled on these? The lines, the cowled folds: elegant beyond anything ever seen on a catwalk or in a magazine.

In every way the scene challenged the senses as I moved through it. The charcoal was aromatic, and the urge to pick up a chunk and bite into it became overwhelming. My mouth watered—and does so now as I recall it. I wanted to put my face to a cob of that burnt wood and take a big bite the way a kid takes a bite from a piece of watermelon. I could imagine the crunch. And my black saliva.

In a way that was wholly celebratory and about relish, I wanted to wear, I wanted to eat, I wanted to take that day into my body.

I wanted to *be* that burnt-out land.

In its extremity, I suppose this could be called a baroque impulse.

IX.

My fallow period lasted five months, coming to a close sooner than I thought it would and undramatically. An outside prompt got me thinking about the essay, a form I'd never considered, and before I knew it, I was writing one.

I have begun to think of the essay as my new frame. In wielding it I feel closest to my camera days. I didn't realise how much I missed it, that restless frame: alighting, adoring, inquiring; ignoring noise and distraction; widening out, zooming in. And moving on.

The viewfinder of the essay may well help me find the missing thing I need to bring back to the novel, but even if it doesn't, it's been useful. It's made obvious to me the tension of the frame, and I find that interesting. Thinking about what it includes, what it excludes; the way the frame nags: by its very existence making us long for a borderless place, where landscape, life and art are indivisible.

•

Back at the football, and still in that first quarter, there's a stoppage in play. I swing my camera back to follow up on the smashed boy, who's been lying on the ground nearby. Kneeling beside him is a trainer.

The van takes my shot.

The trainer gets up and extends his hand. Grasping the man's forearm, the player rises to his feet. Shakes himself off.

The trainer wrenches him to stand still and, with the brusque attention of a rough mother, wipes away the dirt on his temple. The boy spits. Turns. Jogs back to rejoin the action.

The van holds, and as the boy gets further away his form diminishes. My picture, which was filled with his figure, progressively, naturally, becomes a wide shot, showing the far play, the goals, the grandstand. I don't make any move to follow the kid. Leave it wide, this time, to keep everything in.

Then, because it must end the way it always ends, the red light blinks off.

From the Deep, it Comes

The salmon are in. Along the beach the other day rods bent in succession as fishermen reeled them through the waves and up the sand. A pair of young men clutched their strong, kicking fish for photos, excited grins offered to the camera held by a friend. When done, they put their salmon straight in a bucket, not knowing they're a fish that should be bled. If you don't bleed them they taste terrible. If you do bleed them they taste marginally better.

On internet fishing forums advice varies on the best methods for preparing and cooking Australian salmon, but three suggestions are common. 1. Cut salmon into slices, put it on a hook and feed it to a flathead, then eat the flathead. 2. Make salmon into fishcakes, incorporating many other ingredients and serving with chilli sauce so you can't taste the fish. 3. Give it to the cat.

But sharks like salmon. And there's a big possibility that one will be near when there's a school. The other day, just before I walked along the beach to see what the fishermen were catching, I had been swimming.

For many reasons, it's good not to know exactly what's out there.

•

When I was a little girl we went on a family outing to Taronga Park Zoo in Sydney. I remember the elephant but not much else—except the aquarium. I was perhaps six years old, and even then, even to small me, the design of the place seemed foolish.

Raw, knobbly concrete pillars and sculpted, low-arched ceilings were meant to give the appearance of a system of underwater caves, but it was clumsily done, as if someone's uncle had taken up the trowel. Set into the coarse walls were small illuminated tanks which one supposes were intended to look jewel-like, shining out of the gloom, but people had to crowd in close to see anything, and for a child standing well below the required height, glimpses of light and colour were few. When lifted up for a turn at viewing, I could see that the tanks, too, had a homemade appearance: some were empty; some were fogged up; thick gloops of sealant were visible, the efficacy of which was doubtful. This place, which was meant to be so exotic, was already familiar to me: it had the gritty, dank feel of a surf club shower room.

Although I must have seen some fish in those grotto tanks, I don't recall a single one. Maybe an octopus . . . suckers on a reaching arm. But in another section of the aquarium there was a fish that was unforgettable. Unforgettable because it wasn't so much a fish as an observable circumstance—a phenomenon.

It was in the shark pool but it wasn't a shark. The shark pool—the only place big enough to hold my creature—was in a strange building all of its own, the interior structure of which resembled Shakespeare's Globe Theatre. The upper level was a viewing gallery, made of timber and enclosed, except for the balconies that overlooked, and overhung, all four sides of the square pool, seemingly far below. The gallery was supported by piers going down into the water to the floor of the pool, forming a watery cloister. As with the Globe, the centre of the pool was left open to the sky, but despite this natural light, large parts remained in shadow. It was a pit of chiaroscuro.

The pool, which was not very deep, seemed at first to be empty. And then it emerged. From one of the recessed corners it came: a giant stingray. Gliding. Under the overhang of the gallery, past the pilings, it circled the square pool at an unvarying pace. Nearly 2 metres across its disc, it was all black except for a few mottled spots near the raised holes of its eyes. Hardly a lift of its great flaps was required for it to proceed, only an occasional curl—a fluting along the edge—which afforded a glimpse of its snowy-white underneath.

Around and around it went, direction unchanging.

Scattered across the bottom of the pool, like some gypsy mosaic, greenly glinting, were copper and silver coins. Tossed for luck.

Up on the balcony, sitting cross-legged, I watched through the railings, and in one sense would do so all my life.

Magnificent and black and gliding. Into the shadows and out.

Elegant, mad, prisoner.

•

Memories may be potent but of course they can be unreliable. From time to time over the years I have idly researched the history of the zoo to find out about the aquarium, but photographs are few, and I've seen none of the shark pool, so my childhood recollections are hard to check.

The aquarium was built in 1927, and as it turns out the design has been acknowledged as poor, over-influenced by the aesthetic of the Hon. Frederick Flowers: unionist, Labor politician and chairman of the zoo's trustees. The grotto concept, the execution of which Flowers personally supervised, was implemented with remarkable disregard for practical consequences. Plumbing for exhibits in the mock rock of the cave area was located in a crawl space behind the tanks, and small manholes in the concrete above provided the only access for servicing. So tight were these spaces only a little person could use them, and the zoo had to employ an appropriately sized worker to fit.

Structural problems soon surfaced and the roof leaked after only two years. Almost every decade one section or another was shut down for safety reasons, or renovated, or demolished. In 1991 the last of the old aquarium buildings closed.

Stingrays of enormous size certainly were exhibited in the shark pool when opportunity permitted: that is, when someone spotted one in the harbour, where it could feasibly be caught. The first two were captured in 1952 at the Captain Cook graving dock at the naval base on Sydney's Garden Island. Locally they became known as Captain Cook rays, but their more general common name is the smooth stingray (*Dasyatis brevicaudata*). Distributed around three-quarters of the Australian coastline, they are one of the largest stingray species in the world. Offshore they are found down to depths of 170 metres, but they enjoy the shallow waters of harbours, estuaries and coastal bays. It's a thought to lie with in bed at night: while the city of Sydney moves unknowingly above and all about, the big rays are there.

At the graving dock, the rays were found when the water was pumped out. With the aid of a wharf crane, they were lifted out and put on a truck for the zoo. Sir Edward Hallstrom, the zoo's director, was pragmatic about their chances. 'We do not expect them to live for very long,' he told journalists. 'But when they die they will make a grand feed for the zoo's polar bears.'

Hallstrom, who in his professional life manufactured refrigerators, was another enthusiastic zoo amateur with a big personality who treated the place as his own Disneyland.

Despite initially refusing to eat, the largest of the two sting-rays survived for several years and was eventually joined by another from the naval base. But the ray I saw was probably one found in the early 1960s in the harbour pool at Clifton Gardens. A local woman, surmising it had got in under the shark net and couldn't find its way out, reported it to zoo officials. Years later, remembering its lonely existence in the shark pool, she said she regretted her intervention.

Hallstrom was speaking from long experience regarding the shortened lives of many of the zoo's marine animals. During the first few years of the shark pool's operation, nearly all the sharks died within days, prompting the zoo to pay generous rewards to any shark fishermen whose offerings stayed alive past a week. There was no trouble finding replacements. On one weekend alone in 1929, five sharks were brought in by different people, towed in behind boats to the little beach near the zoo's wharf. Several thousand onlookers gathered to watch the landing of the largest, a big tiger shark. A horde of men pitched in to subdue it, passing ropes around it as it thrashed in the shallows; finally they got it onto a truck for the short road trip to the pool.

Survival rates gradually improved for grey nurse sharks, and two individuals managed to live for five and thirteen years respectively, but other species continued to die rapidly. Even taking the attitudes of a different era into account, the zoo's relentless acquisition of sharks seems obtuse, so lacking in appreciation for the animal beyond its function as an attraction as to be a kind of philistinism. Only public complaints about cruelty in the 1950s stopped the zoo advertising payments for capture. Removal of hooks and rough handling during transportation must have caused mortal damage, but the unsuitability of conditions in the pool, though not spoken of, were also surely to blame. My childhood impression of its being quite shallow was correct. It was 7 feet deep.

•

Sleek and powerful, the grey nurse sharks mesmerised one particular visitor to the aquarium in 1936, and he stayed to watch them for hours. It was Zane Grey. He was an American, a novelist, one of the first millionaire authors the world had seen. He was also a big-game fisherman. Like the shark pool and the giant ray I saw in it, Zane Grey has become lodged in my psyche. His restless inquiry into the sea and the creatures in it pre-echoes my obsessions. He's a fascinating figure. For starters, he popularised the Western, writing more than 70 of them, the majority of which were made into movies.

Grey wrote quickly, in longhand, working hard to keep up production while away on the trips he was constantly taking. Weeks or, more often, months were spent apart from his family, hunting, fishing and camping—pursuits he'd enjoyed since boyhood—but several major journeys undertaken between 1908 and 1913, early in his career, became crucial to his writing. Led by expert guides, these were physically taxing and dangerous affairs that took Grey into the desert heart of America to spectacular canyon and mesa country. Some locations, like the Rainbow Bridge National Monument, had only been seen by a handful of white people. Traditionally, these places were respected as so powerful, so forbidding, they were only infrequently visited by the Navajo, or avoided altogether, their mystery and potency thus conserved.

Grey was difficult material as a husband, and not just because of his absences. A loner who nevertheless kept an entourage, he was loyal but not faithful; he was demanding; he suffered bouts of anger and sudden dips in mood. In the outdoors, a need in him for both peace and action seemed to be answered, but whatever the requirements of his soul, on a practical level the wilderness landscapes he observed and the encounters he had in them were worked into his books, giving authenticity to his words. Grey understood the power of truly remote and little-known places, and he understood what it was like to be somewhere and not know what would happen next.

•

In 1918 Grey moved his family from Pennsylvania to California to be near the movie industry and closer to the Pacific Ocean for game fishing. When we think of writers and fishing we think of Hemingway, but he was still in his teens when Zane Grey took up the new sport. It was Grey who first promoted it, sharing his experiences in the countless articles he wrote for outdoor magazines. It was already a rich man's pursuit, especially the way Grey did it, which was to mount and equip his expeditions as if he were an explorer. In fact, he was an explorer, pioneering techniques and finding new fish and fishing grounds. He corresponded widely with scientists, missionaries, market fishermen and sportsmen all around the world to gather information, following up on big fish stories and likely haunts. Grey fished the waters of Florida, Cuba, Mexico and the Galápagos, going to ever more distant places during the 1920s, including Tahiti and New Zealand.

His fishing forays extended as his interest in travelling to the American West diminished. By the end of the decade he vowed he would never go back to Arizona again—it was ruined, he claimed, by the motor car. New roads had opened up the country and it was 'overrun' by tourists. He thought the Navajo doomed. The romance and solitude of the West were lost, he said, without taking into account his own contribution to its demise. It was he, after all, who first exposed the secrets of the place through his bestselling novels. But in any event, he did not need to go back. He had all he required. Those landscapes had become a place in, and of, his imagination, ever productive for him, and mutable, just as the larger myth of 'the West' was to be for generations of Americans—and others too: because it was, of course, an idea that went global.

Grey owned many vessels in his time, and on a trip to New Zealand he commissioned another, the 50-foot *Avalon*, built to his own specifications. He was back home in California when reports came to him of swordfish caught in the relatively un-explored and unfished waters of Australia. A new frontier was on offer, and Grey could not resist. Orders went out for the *Avalon* to cross the Tasman.

Grey arrived in Sydney by passenger liner, to a celebrity's welcome. In his early sixties with thick, silver hair cut in a boyish style, he was vital and attractive. With his wealth, his Hollywood connections and his adventurous intentions, he was an exotic creature himself, and irresistible news. But the sights of the city did not hold him long and he soon headed south by road to meet the *Avalon* at the coastal town of Bermagui. In the seas around Montague Island, where the continental shelf comes closest to the Australian mainland, Grey expected action.

Nothing was done by halves and a substantial beachside camp was established. Personnel included additional boatmen, some with specialist local knowledge, and a camera crew of three for whom a second boat was leased. They would shoot footage for a feature film Grey planned to make on the Great Barrier Reef, but their pictures would be important for another reason. Without pictures, who would believe a fisherman's stories?

For three months the two boats fished off the south coast, and big game was plentiful. Grey caught marlin and sharks, some so rarely hooked at that time that they were difficult to identify: one, a green thresher shark, was the first ever known to be captured. Grey's most significant catch was a yellowfin tuna. Although vast schools of these fish appeared each year, they had never been properly identified. Grey alerted locals to a valuable fishery they hadn't known to harvest.

Content with his catch, Grey moved north, stopping off in Sydney briefly on the way to Queensland. In Sydney, the idea came to him that he'd like to be the first person to catch a marlin off the Heads. What an arresting photo it would make—in the foreground a leaping fish, and behind it the harbour entrance, the city and even the curve of the new Harbour Bridge.

For two days he and his crew caught nothing. Some hours into the third morning they hooked a small bronze whaler and cut it up for bait, hoping to attract something much bigger. As Grey tells the story in his book *An American Angler in Australia*, the day was hot and the sea blue and a lazy mood settled over the boat. There were no bites. Lunch was served and the table cleared away. The crew dozed. Hours slipped by but Grey was content watching the water and the birds; he stayed in his fishing chair. Dreamy but attuned.

By four o'clock in the afternoon and still with no bites, the crew were bored, ready to give up and go home. But Grey demurred, mildly reproaching them, reminding them of the time he fished for 83 days without a bite before catching a giant Tahitian striped marlin on the eighty-fourth. The boatmen, the camera boys, he was paying their wages. There was no question of any real dissent. He was the boss. But it was clear to Grey his crew thought staying on was a waste of time. He said no more to convince them but settled in his chair. A feeling of sureness was growing in him. Something was out there. It was as if, in his state of languid alertness, he was calling it up. Patiently creating the right conditions for it to arrive.

And then it happened. Slowly but firmly the line on Grey's reel began to pull out. He told his head boatman it was like nothing he'd ever felt before, like someone with their fingers on his coat sleeve drawing him slowly towards them. In this inexorable way, 400 metres of line were taken in no time. Grey struck, then reeled in slack, fast and hard. When he came upon the full weight of the fish the response was so violent it lifted him clear of his chair.

What sort of fish it was they couldn't tell, but they knew it wasn't a marlin. Its behaviour was changeable. For a while it went light, then it went heavy; heavy in the way of something more than ordinarily huge. Forced after one run to apply more drag on his reel than he'd ever done in his life, Grey thought it must be a shark, but maybe a species no one had ever seen.

With the creature taking line and Grey struggling to get it back, the fight seesawed, becoming more and more operatic as the afternoon wore on, played out just as Grey originally envisaged, albeit with a different fish, in front of one of the world's great backdrops. Sunset came, lighting the sandstone cliffs of the Heads and turning the sea to Egyptian gold-blue. And when the sky further darkened, three towering ocean liners, with lights glittering, passed within 100 metres of Grey's boat on their way out of port.

Just as the battle between man and fish reached a desperate stage, the revolving beam of the nearby lighthouse at Watsons Bay switched on, raking the *Avalon*'s deck and surrounding ocean.

Grey, drawing on his last reserves of energy, got back more line, and when finally the leader of the line sprang into view, men leapt to action and adrenaline surged. Beside the boat the water boiled then split open to show the wide flat back of an enormous shark, pearl grey in colour, with dark tiger stripes and a huge rounded head. Grey, expecting a hideous beast, was shocked by its beauty.

Amid churning water and roaring shouts the shark rolled, showing its white belly and opening its mouth wide enough to take a barrel, before snapping its jaws audibly shut.

Grey had a rod-fishing world record. When measured, the tiger shark was 13 feet 10 inches long. It weighed 1036 pounds.

•

Zane Grey considered himself part of the quest for knowledge. He revered the natural world and spent his life contemplating the majesty of wild places and things, about which much was still unknown. What might he bring up from the sea next? Great white sharks and tiger sharks were known to grow to 20 feet, but stories came to him of monsters far exceeding this: sharks bigger than the boats of commercial fishermen; a 39-foot great white sighted near Montague Island; dredged-up teeth from the ocean floor so big that one scientist calculated they must belong to a shark of 80 feet or more. Grey wrote, 'The waters around Australia are alive with many species of sharks. Why not some unknown species, huge and terrible? Who can tell what forms of life swim and battle in ocean depths?' With the enthusiasm of a zealot he said, *I believe*.

I believe there are eighty-foot sharks. Rare, surely, but they occur . . . It takes imagination to be a fisherman—to envision things and captures to be. Every fisherman, even if he is a sceptic and ridicules me and my supporters about these great fish, betrays himself when he goes fishing, for he surely goes because he imagines there are trout or salmon or Marlin, and surely a big one, waiting to strike for him.

Zane Grey was not just a fisherman, he was a writer. He knew about imagination. He had fished within sight of a modern city and brought something huge and fearsome and wonderful out of the waters, first divining its presence where there was no evidence for it, and when others doubted the possibility.

In his day, still so brimming with mystery, it would seem inconceivable to most people that only one long lifetime later the seas around the world would be not only raked over and used up in innumerable ways, but also in parts significantly destroyed. But Grey had an inkling it might happen: cases of overfishing by commercial operators already had him worried, and he urged sport fishermen to practise catch-and-release once self-imposed quotas were reached. He had seen it before: the unstoppable march of people marring the purity of wilderness landscapes.

•

Today, there are almost no hidden places left in the natural world to discover, though our requirement for the wonder they furnish goes undiminished. Cognisant of this, perhaps we should be more protective of our own internal spaces, for it may be that these last deeps are also endangered. We have psycho-analysed our minds, mapped our brains with imaging machines, sought constant stimulation for our grey matter, seemingly afraid to let our heads go quiet for a minute. But we need our private recesses in order to survive well, and to create. In those deeps imagination lives. Awe reposes. A strange alchemy takes place there: present experience mixes with memory, and associations knit. It's a process that's resistant to inquiry and logical sense, but rising up out of that waiting space, something marvellous or roaring or provoking might come: an image, an idea, or both merged as one. The new thing.

I believe.

And so it is I let memory and imagination go, and metaphors mix. And it comes to me. Why should the aquarium of my childhood not change, the shark pool become, instead, the Pantheon in Rome—flooded?

In shallow water, over the marble floor, my stingray gliding. Around and around. Snow drifting down from the oculus. The giant ray passing in silence by Raphael's tomb.

For what is a pantheon, if not a zoo for gods?

The Tomb of Human Curiosity

It's 3 am. The front deck of the house and the road beyond are a silver gelatin photograph—fine-grained, sharply delineated, seven different shades of monochrome. I could step out there right now and perform any daytime activity: mow the lawn or ride a bicycle. Instead I pad to the bathroom and back. In a few hours my brother and I will get up to go tide-hunting.

The moon, spreading her unordinary grey light, has everything to do with our plans.

•

The alarm goes off. Coffee. I move quietly about, pausing again at the glass sliding door to check the weather and the state of the bay at the end of the street. It's overcast, a light

85

breeze, but the prediction is for sun later. Sun and no wind are what we need for optimum viewing.

Back to bed for a short read. Just as long as it takes to drink the coffee.

Roger has come last night from Melbourne and I want to let him sleep for a bit. Though I feel like an impatient child on Christmas morning, there's really no need to rush. Phase one is not time critical as long as we launch the boat in the next two hours, and phase two will not happen until after lunch.

We've wanted to do this for a long time—experience a low low tide while out on the water—and talking over the phone ten days ago got serious enough to check our commitments and calendars against tide charts, only to find the best opportunity in the next three months was soon. Quickly we made the most important arrangements: Rog booked a flight and I bought a bathyscope.

I suppose few 56-year-old women yearn for a bathyscope, but I have rarely felt more cheerful than when I brought mine home. Looking like a big orange traffic cone, it's a refined version of a glass-bottomed bucket. It has a handle, so the viewer can lean over the side of the boat and tilt it into the surface of the water, and it's tapered so you may, if you wish, put your face to the narrowed end, blocking out extraneous light.

A simple, well-made object, the bathyscope promised

something impressive and secret beyond itself. It was a spy-hole into another realm. But at low tide, what is newly above the water is just as interesting as what is below, so using the scope was only part of our expedition.

We wanted to see it all: the waterway of our childhood drained and transformed.

·

You'd think we'd have witnessed it before, but our custom was to only fish the high end of the rising tide. By repute, this is the best time to fish, but it's also the only time I can easily get out on the water. My little dinghy can only be launched from the foreshore where it's kept when enough water creeps in over the mudflats. I fish always with one eye on the clock, mindful of having enough water to get back in. A rookie miscalculation in the distant past was a humiliating lesson I swore not to repeat. Half sobbing, I had to drag the boat across mud, sinking up to my knees, fretful I would be stuck myself. It was hardly a life-threatening situation, as my struggle was played out in full sight of the road, but for a shy person that was almost the worst part. The stupid truth is, I would rather have died than been helped.

Tidal effects on the inlet where the family holiday shack is located tend to the dramatic because of the local geography. The water system is complicated. From the bar at the ocean mouth through to the broadwater upstream, the water pours through channels, past sandbars and mangrove islands, into bays deep and shallow, repeatedly squeezing and spreading between landforms. My brother and I find the movements fascinating. How could we not, having both, as children, daydreamed on wharves, watching the current slide by, forever making then undoing itself in paisley whorls. We did not understand the exaggerating influence of different phases of the moon, but loved the periodic high high of spring tides when the lower landings of the wharves were underwater and the world seemed drowned, and when, on the corresponding low lows, the shoreline extended impossibly and oyster leases rose up, exposed. Discussing it over the years, we often remarked on our continuing ignorance, for as adults we still had only the sketchiest grasp of the physical laws governing this phenomenon, though it must rank as one of the planet's most fundamental. This seemed inexcusable to us when we lived so intimately with the inlet when we holidayed, and when, right in front of our eyes, the tides went on with their obvious business.

Now, finally, we were stirring ourselves to learn more. This time we were determined to see the other half of the show in detail. Our plan was to survey my usual territory to see what we could of the seafloor and underwater life while the inlet was shallowest, and to observe any other changes above the surface. We really had no clear expectations of the trip beyond adding to our personal body of knowledge about the estuary.

But first we had to solve the problem of getting out in the boat. Although we might have made the trip without fuss in a hire boat from the marina, we scorned this as a buying of experience, as well as a betrayal of my beaten-up but much-loved vessel, the *Squid*. No—with scheming, teamwork and a tolerant approach to the probable inconveniences, we would overcome any logistical obstacles ourselves.

While I like to do lots of things by myself, I knew this investigation would be all the easier and better if undertaken with Rog. He's cheerful and confident, interested in everything and, like the schoolteacher he once was, loves a practical lesson. His knowledge is wide and useful, and taking after our long-gone engineer father, he relishes the puzzle of any problem, breaking it down into components.

For all these reasons it would be good to have him with me, but mostly I valued his presence for his enthusiasm. Bring him something to marvel over and he'll unfailingly oblige. After due admiration, he's likely to assume a thoughtful pose, putting a hand to his close-cropped white beard while tilting his head for a fresh view out of his glasses. Then he'll ask a question on an aspect of the marvel I hadn't considered.

A pleasant half-hour is bound to ensue as we kick around possible answers. As the middle sibling, he's older than me by a couple of years, but he never takes over. Instead, our mutual understanding of the subject at hand is likely to be enlarged or, at the very least, our appreciation of what we do not understand improved. Afterwards the marvel is returned unharmed.

The previous night, when we talked of our outing, we'd been equals in our excitement. It was laughable how long we discussed the sequence of our tasks and timings, checking and rechecking the tide chart and weather forecasts—cross-referencing with apps. Though we were hardly preparing for a rocket launch to Pluto, we felt intrepid, and madly pleased with ourselves.

Prompted by his study of the chart, Rog asked an apparently simple question. Why are there two tides a day in most places, while in a few, seemingly random places, there is only one?

For the past week or so I'd been doing our homework, so I was prepared. But when I embarked on an explanation of the multiple, interlinking factors behind 'tidal bulges', it soon became obvious the details were beyond me. I didn't feel bad about my defeat.

Nothing's straightforward when it comes to tides, I told him. So much so that an ancient philosopher, exhausted by the complications and anomalies which he encountered, once described the study of tides as 'the tomb of human curiosity'.

'Wow,' said Rog.

•

On the morning high we work well together as we launch the boat, stowing the few pieces of essential gear previously agreed upon. Rog climbs in first. Standing beside the boat in water just over my knees, I lean in to start the motor. Coughs of blue smoke and a rough idle until it warms up.

I wade out with the boat a little further then hop in myself—a deft movement, I like to think, which also involves quickly flicking the motor into gear, then just as quickly leaning my weight towards the bow, thus lifting the stern a few inches higher to give the prop more clearance as we cross the shallows. When the water deepens I can relax, drop the leg of the motor fully down and rip the throttle to full bore. It's a 3.5-horsepower engine, so we're not exactly flying, but we grin.

We pass by the cluster of moored boats in the bay and along the remaining line of sticks marking an old oyster lease. A hill shelters us from the breeze, so the water here is smooth and clear. Perhaps 4 metres beneath us is a broad belt of the seagrass I call ribbon weed, growing in dark health. As we look down, skimming over it, we're greedy for it. It makes us smack our lips for what the afternoon might bring.

Our trip is a short one and though we're tempted to extend it (because the same sudden good feeling at being out on the water again has rushed over both of us), we stick to our plan. I steer in to our destination, a public wharf which is not much visited on a weekday, and which is only ten minutes' walk from home. Rog runs a rope through a railing on the lower landing and we begin the business of tying up. We do a secure job of it, with Rog reminding me we need to pay out enough rope to accommodate the dropping water level. The tide will fall over 1.6 metres.

At any sudden movement or weight-shift, the *Squid* tips and tilts dangerously, so we're careful as we go about our unloading tasks, always telling each other in advance of our intentions so the other will automatically act to counterbalance. We leave nothing in the boat but the motor, which I padlock. We're done. We'll come back in six hours and twelve and a half minutes. That's when the tide will be dead low.

That's when phase two will begin.

•

When I did my homework on tides, I tracked historical developments in thinking. Even though Isaac Newton was the breakthrough man, the one to correctly theorise that the combined gravity of the moon and the sun was the force pulling on oceans, it was his predecessor, Galileo, who snagged my attention.

As a boy, Galileo considered becoming a painter. The natural artistic ability he possessed was put to good use when, years later, he tilted the new technology of his telescope to the night sky to draw the phases of the moon.

He didn't know it, but at the same time an Englishman, Thomas Harriot, was also experimenting with a telescope and training it moonwards. The Englishman made a drawing too, but it was a crude map, never published in his lifetime. Galileo's drawings are of a whole different order, naturalistically reproducing what he saw, with more than ordinary skill. In a sequence of inky skies there is the modern moon as we know it—that rough golf ball—variously shaded, its cold topography finally revealed.

What's difficult to believe is that no one before Galileo had drawn the moon as they saw it: all known public or published depictions predating his are in one way or another symbolic. Throughout human history the dings and spots on the moon visible to the naked eye had gone unrecorded. It makes these first images of Galileo's all the more haunting—how lucky we are they are also art. A creative confidence is apparent in their execution, but, more than that, an appreciative respect for the moon's austerity is also communicated.

Galileo's telescope was not very sophisticated. It only brought us a little closer. His great achievement was to show us what was already in plain view.

•

Galileo's observations of the moon and other heavenly bodies led him to believe the earth rotated, causing a shifting of the world's waters in their basins, which generated tides. His proofs concerning the rotation of the earth supported the Copernican theory of the heavens—a dangerous theory to promote. Catholic authorities had burnt the astronomer Giordano Bruno at the stake for holding similar views, so when the Inquisition began to investigate Galileo, the seriousness of his predicament was not in doubt.

Copernican theory contradicted the received thinking of centuries, but worse, it hinted at an impersonal universe, ungoverned. Man, labouring on a planet which was no longer central to the system, seemed incidental. This first glimpse of cosmic loneliness must have sent people reeling, but for the Church the problem was also political, calling into question its right to temporal power.

Threatened with torture, Galileo recanted, but this didn't save him from further punishment. A sentence of life imprisonment was commuted to house arrest and his remaining years were spent in a villa outside Florence, where he was forbidden to work.

•

Though closely supervised in his imprisonment, Galileo had one visitor in 1638. It was the English poet John Milton, author-to-be of *Paradise Lost*. We know this because Milton records the bare fact of their interview in a tract he wrote defending free speech. Milton was 30 years old. The elderly astronomer was lonely and ill, and almost totally blind. I find the idea of their encounter compelling, coincidentally because Milton was already on my mind in relation to tides, but also because I think of the occasion as youth meeting age, as poetry meeting science. If anyone could fully appreciate the tragedy of a questing mind denied the chance to roam, it would be a writer.

In his own cosmos of *Paradise Lost*, Milton honoured Galileo with a place, the only contemporary figure to be mentioned in the poem. He describes the shield Satan wears as hanging on his shoulders like the moon,

. . . whose orb
Through optic glass the Tuscan artist views
At evening, from the top of Fesolè,

Or in Valdarno, to descry new lands,
Rivers, or mountains, in her spotty globe.

Paradise Lost was published in 1667.

It would be another twenty years before Isaac Newton
recognised the true power of the spotty globe to steer the seas,
giving Rog and me the low low we desired.

•

At low tide, what I expected to see and what I *hoped* to see were two
different things. All along when planning this enterprise, I secretly
thought I'd see something biblical—something Miltonian. In
Paradise Lost, the archangel Raphael tells Adam about the creation
of the world and describes God commanding life into the oceans.
To half quote, half paraphrase, God says that forthwith the seas,
the creeks and bays will swarm with innumerable fry. Fish 'with
their Finns and shining Scales' will glide under the green wave in
banks of schools, they will 'Graze the Sea-weed, their pasture, and
through Groves of Coral stray, or sporting with quick glance, show
to the Sun their waved coats dropped with Gold'.

Shellfish in pearly shells are mentioned, crustaceans in
jointed armour, seals, dolphins, whales.

Somehow I half believed the contents of Milton's beautiful
teeming sea would be thickly visible when low tide reduced

the estuary's channels to gutters. All life poured in there and flapping. Hardly enough water left for them to breathe. Pink snapper, parrotfish and bream, brown-striped trumpeter, dory and shovel-nosed sharks, pineapple fish and prawns, blennies and gobbies, squid, bonito and yellowtail, scaly mackerel, octopus, flounder, flathead, leatherjacket, morwong, whiting, blue swimmer crab, rock cod, wrasse and more besides. They could not all ride the ebb out to sea. Surely, on a low low, with so little water left, the reduced passageways might be mythically populated with rivers of fish?

·

After lunch we pack the bathyscope into the car, along with fishing gear and all the other stuff we didn't feel it was wise to leave in the boat while waiting for the tide to fall. We drive around to the wharf, which juts out from a thin band of mangroves growing close to the road. The wharf stands knobble-kneed, arthritic with encrustations of oysters on its pilings. As we get out of the car the aromatics of the ecosystem hit us—an iron, mollusc smell, tinged with an under-scent of rottenness, yet lung-floodingly wholesome.

At the start of the wharf we pause to listen to the crackle of the silty mud releasing air from the many little crab and worm holes. Between the upright fingers of the mangroves' pneumatophores, a few tiny grey crabs sidle, but we see no other creatures as we cart our things up the wharf, though we look carefully, noting the subtle changes as the water gradually deepens. In the first, fully exposed zone, a few dotted clumps of pop-weed grow—their leathery beads, filled with water, must help them withstand the drying. And then, in puddled water, the short eelgrass starts, though it looks collapsed and gasping. After that, the ribbon grass begins, just as soon as the water is deep enough to offer at least partial support for its strap leaves, which can grow over half a metre long. In fact, strap weed is its correct common name, but the labels of childhood stick fast.

Fortune has smiled on us. On this warm afternoon in late October, the water is clear and the cloud cover has burnt off to leave us with plenty of blue sky. Conditions are close to peak.

As it happens, we weren't so smart after all with our boat tie-up, but it's only a minor setback. A change in wind direction has jammed the boat partially underneath the main landing, wedging it in the oystery grasp of a couple of pilings. No choice but to wrench the *Squid* free. The brittle edges of the shells crumble as the gunwales of the boat grind against them, and I wince, not out of regret for any probable worsening of the boat's appearance, but out of sympathy for the imagined pain inflicted on my trusty fibreglass friend.

We are careful lowering ourselves down into the tippy boat, but once each of us commits, the downward pressure on the hull is sudden and I privately worry how my DIY fibreglass patches will hold up, especially given the man-size of Rog. He's tall but also carries a bit more weight than is healthy for his heart, which concerns me. Our dad died of a cardiac arrest at much the same age Rog is now.

In the event, we get ourselves in without mishap and the *Squid* stays watertight. Rog puts on his new sunglasses, which he calls his old bastards' sunnies. They fit over his normal spectacles, so they're not exactly cool, but he cheerfully declares he doesn't give a rat's. They're polarised so he'll be able to see into the water beyond the glare. He's also wearing a seaman's peaked cap over his short, snowy white hair, but I don't think his choice of headgear is intentionally nautical, because I've seen him wear it to the shops. My own *Squid* fashions are not exactly haute: an ancient maroon t-shirt; shorts, clean but marked by previous boating trips; a baby-blue baseball cap embroidered with *Davistown Putt Putt Regatta*. We're a right pair.

We set off.

Immediately, we're onstage. Crowning up out of the middle of the bay ahead of us is the biggest oyster lease, about 2 hectares in area. Beyond it, the estuary widens, the channels carving their way left towards the ocean; to our right, up the waterway, is the Rip Bridge, past which the water splits into multiple arms, all beyond the normal operating range of the *Squid*. The steepness of the hills near us, and in the distance in their sloping layers of hazy eucalypt greys, adds to the psychology of low tide, making the idea of the draining of the trough of the estuary seem all the more striking.

We turn the boat into the nearby channel—a favoured stretch of mine for fishing—and slow up, ready to look for the first time through the bathyscope.

•

What we see is nothing.

For all the hours of that long afternoon, the bathyscope reveals cool, lovely emptiness. No creatures. No Miltonian rivers of fish, not even what I had realistically expected: the odd, igniting glimpse of something swimming along the bottom.

Whatever hasn't been disgorged into the ocean is certainly well hidden, or nowhere near us.

•

We conduct our survey work first, travelling the length of the sandy-bottomed strip between the lease and the shore, checking each edge in turn to see where the weed bellies out and in. By the changing colour we can tell the difference in the bottom with the naked eye, but with the bathyscope we have detail. The sand is pocked and deserted; flecks of nutriment drift between it and the bathyscope glass in a grand sweep of particles. The ribbon weed is downy with algal growth, and some of its brown-green leaves are also flecked with a kind of white hoar. No fish from *Paradise Lost* graze over it, or nudge between its fronds.

We move into Rileys Bay and motor into the corner where the bush comes down to mangroves and a tidal flat. Between that shore and us is a large meadow of seagrass—the ubiquitous ribbon weed again—starting in shallow water and growing out into deeper. I cut the motor and we nose in. In perhaps half a metre of water we drift over the meadow.

We are somewhere magical.

Thriving on the increased sun and freer of algae, some of the leaves are lime green. They bend over at the surface, but wherever tiny edges pierce the surface tension, light catches, so that we sit in an acre of sparkles.

The bathyscope adds another dimension to the experience, taking us closer—like Galileo's telescope—inside the meadow, the grasses nodding and parting to the slow advance of the glass. A couple of times we disturb a strange brown fish seeming to sunbake on the surface, but each flips away at great speed before we can see it properly. Other than that, we see only a few whelk shells, grey with sediment, resting at the base of grasses. Reflected onto the green mat of the meadow is the transparent blue film of the sky, and so it simultaneously seems we are gliding through water and air.

We stay there for a long time. It's hard to drag ourselves away.

At one point I tell Rog that right up until the Middle Ages many people believed tides were caused by the world breathing in and out.

There in the ribbon grass meadow, that explanation makes perfect sense to us both.

•

When we return to our planned work we chug around to the far side of the big lease to explore the bottom there, then we head off to the sandbars. What surprises me is that several are already submerged. From the shore at low tide, it seems like they're all high and dry for hours.

Pleasure boats the size of small ships come uncomfortably close in the narrow channels, so we skedaddle. We can't go home—not enough water there—so we head off to experiment with fishing the rising low.

•

We take up our customary drift, and although the line of it is hard to hold with the breeze picking up, we at once get bites. Hard to believe when not long before all signs of fishy life had been absent.

After an hour or so we've got a feed of big whiting and Rog has caught a nice flathead. We anchor to try for crabs. There's no action but we don't care. We settle in for the wide-ranging chat we couldn't have when busy earlier.

We talk about Roger's grown-up son, Carl, who lives in Canada, and whose wedding we'd been to four months earlier. I felt for my brother and sister-in-law that day as they gave away their only child to another country, to another family eager to take him over. Though it was obvious how much their son meant to them, they did not speak of any loss to themselves, but showed only a fierce pride in his happiness, and confidence in the future he'd chosen. Rog was subdued, though not in a manner that drew the attention of others. I only knew it myself because I've seen him go that way once or twice before in times of great moment. Right now he's his usual self, chirping away, telling me Carl has been to the famous Bay of Fundy in Nova Scotia, where the world's biggest tides rush in and out, rising a whopping 14 metres. I shake off my memories of the wedding reception and of Rog struggling to manage the complex feelings of the occasion, and I join in.

That's nothing, I tell him. You wouldn't believe the monstrous sweep of tides when the earth was young. And away I go on an explanation which has to be told in careful steps, but it's worth it to get to some boggling concepts.

When the world began, I lecture, the moon was closer and the earth rotated faster, which sent the waters of the oceans tearing backwards and forwards in tides of unimaginable reach and ferocity. Gradually the moon receded, ironically because of the tides themselves. Their movement takes energy out of the earth, slowing its rotation, and that energy goes into the moon's orbit, making it bigger. So, as the moon travels around us, it's gradually getting further away, and as the moon becomes more distant, the tidal effect on the earth is lessened.

The moon won't keep going and going though, because it's estimated that in about 50 billion years the moon and the earth will go into tidal lock, having reached a state where effects equal out. But well before that could ever happen, in just a measly 2.3 billion years, the sun's radiation will evaporate the oceans. There'll be no more tides then. And probably not much of anything else.

That's what you get if you follow the tides to their scientific end—fried.

But, Rog and I agree, chances are high we'll fry ourselves long before the cosmos gets around to doing it for us.

•

As we talk we check the baits on the crab lines and continue to fish with our rods. And then I notice something. It's about 10 metres away and backlit in the afternoon sun, so I can't make it out well, but it looks like a floating beer can. I'm thinking we should go and scoop it up. And then it sinks. Strange. Then it bobs up again—

'Rog! A turtle, a turtle's head!'

And so it is. The blunt, block head sinks and rises once more, as if it needs to take another look at us to be sure of something, then it sinks for the last time. Off it swims, the wider, brown-yellow shape of its shell discernible under the water for a moment until it disappears.

If I had not seen a turtle swimming in the bay a couple of years ago I would never have identified this rare visitor in the difficult light.

Having just contemplated the end of the world, we are immensely cheered by the turtle's appearance. Not yet, not yet, it seems to say. Yet the preciousness of its presence is chastening.

•

The afternoon is passing; I put away my rod and begin cleaning our catch while Rog fishes on. He mentions a boyhood excursion to Fort Denison, the little island in the middle of Sydney Harbour, topped with the familiar pepper pot of its Martello tower. I had been there myself only a few days before, because it houses something I wouldn't mind having in my own home—a tide room. Which is why Rog brought it up, of course.

His visit is news to me, but I can easily picture him trudging around in his cubs' uniform with the slightly baffled look on his face that was his usual expression until our parents finally twigged that he couldn't see properly and got him glasses.

Nothing much about the tide room could have changed in the many years between our visits. Extending out into the harbour off the western side of the tower, it is much as you would like it to be. It has sandstone walls, arrow-slit windows and a seaweed smell. But there the romance ends. It's empty, except for a few bits of junky-looking equipment arranged close to a hole in the floor, which is covered by a scratched piece of perspex. Though a spotlight blasts on it, you cannot see the water down there. Nor can you hear it gurgle or slop as you'd wish. A long dipstick is stashed at the end of the room, and though it would be nice to feed it into the hole and do a little measuring of one's own, this is obviously not allowed.

Predictions for tides all along the New South Wales coast are made based on the measurements taken here. This is literally ground zero for New South Wales tides, and has been since 1857, when a benchmark was cut into the outer wall of the tower. Tides are recorded as so many millimetres above or below a zero. But the zero is arbitrary. It's just a mark at an accessible point that can be easily observed. As a sign of human agency and ingenuity it's so basic it's inspiring; a scratched statement of will towards the understanding of something immense.

But like so many marks and places in Australia, there are underlying, under-told stories. Before it was used as a gaol by the colonists and razed for a fort, the island was a natural jewel in the harbour. Rising out of the deep water, it was a tall, interesting knob of grey rock, dotted with twisted trees and shrubs. It was an important place for Eora women, those first fishers of Sydney Harbour, who must have possessed a whole other rich bank of knowledge about tides, and the creatures who swam in their rising and falling.

At the tide room, measurements are now taken electronically and read remotely, but alongside the new device are two old machines still in working order. One uses a system where a float is attached by a rod to a pen, which is poised over a turning drum loaded with chart paper. With the spidery finger of the pen, the tide draws itself.

I think some clever artist should make an artwork employing the same principle. Let the stretching sea paint itself, or make music. I'd like to hear the harmonic dictation of tides.

•

It's still pleasant and sunny in this last gilded hour of the afternoon, but we've been on the water in our little boat for many hours and the making tide has now delivered enough water for us to go home.

I pick up a crab line to reel it in but it's heavy with something on it, something much bigger than a crab. Maybe a flattie. Rog gets the landing net ready but soon we can see the form of something we probably won't want in the boat. It's like a stingray, but neither of us has seen one of this type before. It's about 45 centimetres long with two flat lobes of fins beside a short tail. The orange colour of its skin is strange, and the texture rubbery, like an old wetsuit—not the usual sandpaper of a ray. I manage to flip it over and hold it against the gunwale of the boat, exposing its white underbelly and crescent mouth. Luckily the hook comes out easily and the fish slips back into the water, vanishing quickly.

Later, when we looked it up in my sea fishes book, we found out it was a numbfish. Initially the name made sense—as something to do with the rubbery skin. But as I read on, sharing the information with Rog, it soon became apparent the skin had nothing to do with it. The numbfish is capable of delivering an electric shock of more than 200 volts. That's roughly the equivalent of house power. Fishermen have reported excruciating pain and temporary paralysis of limbs when shocked.

I wished I'd looked at it longer, even though I couldn't believe how fortunate I was not to have paid a nasty price for the limited viewing I had.

Numbfish have large expandable mouths. They send a charge out into the water to shock their prey as it passes, then quickly eat it whole. Their usual diet is crabs, fish and worms, but small penguins and even rats have been found in their stomachs. Shocks from numbfish washed up on beaches have been known to travel through wet sand, and poking them with a wet stick is also ill advised. Another common name for the numbfish is the coffin ray.

We call it quits and I drop Rog off at the wharf so he can drive the car around to our home shore while I motor on to meet him there. It's well past six o'clock. We've been out on the water in the little old *Squid* for over five hours. We're thirsty, and stiff from sitting, but in all that time we weren't bored for a minute. We load the outboard, the bathyscope and everything else into the car to transport it the short distance home. I tie the *Squid* off on a tree root at the bank and leave it to bob on the nearly high water.

•

When Rog leaves two days later, I sit at the table in the long verandah room of the holiday house, surrounded by my marine books. The house is quiet. The flurry of activity is over. All our talk, the science, the things we saw, bump like flotsam around me. I wait, letting everything sink and settle, to see if some plain things can be said as a result of our expedition.

We paid careful attention to the tidal changes in the estuary, and new parts of our place opened up to us as a consequence; we saw things that made us love it all the more. But overarching that, I think it's the 'action' of nature which has struck me most forcefully, and as a fresh insight. Without favour and, mercifully, without prejudice, the elastic embrace of nature opens and closes around us all the time. In every locality, even in urban settings where nature struggles on, there's a network of animation with its own rhythms happening right under our noses, to which we're largely oblivious. Few of us rely on that kind of physical awareness anymore to get by on a practical level, but I count it as a lost competency and, further, an eroding factor in the quality of our lives.

Being more attuned to the rich functioning of my surroundings these past few days, I have felt as if I've been living properly in the world for the first time, and an integral part of that has been the human element we've brought to it—the family memories, facts, history, culture. It's this layered knowledge, *combined* with alert attention, which gives the everyday places we inhabit their true dimensionality, which switches them on, turning them fully alive.

I think, for example, of Galileo's moon and all I have learnt of it this past while. From now on, when I'm in the city taking the garbage out to the bins after dinner, I will pause for a moment to search for it in the night sky. I will remember the number of hours and minutes that make up a lunar day; or estimate the strength of its pull on the inlet and see, in my mind's eye, the corresponding look of the evening shore; or I might imagine Aboriginal women paddling their *nowies* under its light, little fires burning brightly in the slim vessels; I will remember the moon as Milton's great ornament and then my rivers of fish, adding a coffin ray to the list. I will look at the grey craters where man has stood and recall the martyr who first drew them.

All of this knowledge quickens the world for me and connects me to the others who share it. And I, in turn, am vivified.

This is belonging.

If we knew our planet's stories as ours, if we twitched to its shifting and sighing, it would hurt us to do it harm.

•

To continue the process of mental sorting, I load the photos I took on our expedition onto my computer. Put them in a folder marked *Low Tide 2016*. Me clowning around in the kitchen at home with the bathyscope; Fort Denison and the tide room. Lots of shots of the seagrass meadow in the corner at Rileys: green straps curving over beneath the thin, butane reflection of sky. Rog—wearing a long-sleeved shirt and soft, old cotton trousers rolled up—sitting on the little seat in the bow of the boat, leaning over with the bathyscope. Then a sequence of him turning to me and reeling back with a roar of laughter so hearty it includes a clichéd slap on the knee. I don't recall what was said. I wish I did. In the next frame he returns his attention to the bathyscope and the grasses. So much going on in a single minute, each of those frames 3.05 pm, 3.05 pm, 3.05 pm, 3.05 pm.

At 3.05 pm, a minute I don't even remember, we could not be happier.

I play the sequence over and over. The luckiness of it, the transience of it. It's mesmerising. In all the rest of our lives, if that was the happiest minute each of us lived, we could not reasonably be disappointed.

With a surge that in its own way is deep and tidal, emotion constricts my throat. There must come the day when only one of us remains to look at these pictures. If it is me, they will undo me.

I ring Rog up that evening and I tell him, 'You wouldn't believe what I've found out about those grasses.'

'That's so good,' he says, approving of the impulse to study that subject too. 'Because remember how that was our best? That was the thing we loved the best?'

It was.

If there is one thing I have discovered for sure from my low tide studies, it is that what is in plain sight is often the most mysterious and astonishing.

I put the phone down.

3.05 pm.

3.05 pm.

3.05 pm.

In those photos, in a garden of ribbon grass—at low tide—I am shocked to find out how much I love my brother.

•

A few weeks later it's Roger's birthday. In a large yellow envelope I send him a half-dried strand of ribbon weed, *Posidonia australis*, an identifying characteristic of which is its rounded tip, perfect, like a guitarist's fingernail. Another thing I'd never noticed before.

On the back of the otherwise empty envelope, I write, *This is your birthday card.*

He'll understand.

He'll like it.

This marvel of ours.

Amateur Hour at the Broken Heart Welding Shop

I've always been attracted to stories of enthusiastic amateurs, self-taught eccentrics with an inexplicable keenness for a chosen field. What I didn't realise until recently is that's because I'm one. I don't know why I've been so slow on the uptake, or what finally brought it home, but I readily admit to it now. Notwithstanding certain drawbacks built into the condition, my amateur rank is even a mild source of pride, because it's long been my belief that there's a niche usefulness in the barminess of amateur thinking which contributes to the enrichment of humankind. At the very least, its half-baked notions entertain and its hopefulness serves to encourage others. Though more often than not the amateur fails to snatch victory from the jaws of defeat, by example they declare that to try and try again is a stimulating pleasure, and (almost) enough reward in itself. With the nobility of a peasant, the amateur persists.

My grandfather was a first-class amateur.

You wouldn't think of amateurism as genetic, but now I've reassessed myself, nothing else explains the gentle brand of crackpotdom we share: I didn't see him very often after I turned seven, and he died when I was twelve, so nurture can hardly be the cause.

While I am an amateur writer, my grandfather was an amateur engineer. Metalwork was his chief love, but he was versatile. At his eightieth birthday party he said in a speech (I have a typed copy of it, and in his short sentences his German accent is somehow embedded): 'I am still making new ideas and tools. I am still not a millionaire. Well, who wants to be?'

Cheerfully he told his guests, 'If anyone is dissatisfied I came into their life, don't blame me, blame the man in the moon, who controlled my destiny.'

As a seventeen year old, running away for the second time in his short life, he tried to stow away on a ship bound for New York but forgot to factor in the tide. Missing his chance to sneak onboard, he eventually ended up in Australia two years later.

A certain amount of bungling is the hallmark of amateurs. By necessity they follow their own instincts, often with mixed consequences. But Pa's amateurism was not voluntary like mine. It was forced on him by his father, who perversely refused to let him train as an engineer, even when there was easy means.

While it may not have been much of a comfort to Pa, the recompense for having to scrape together his own knowledge was that he was never bound by professional orthodoxies, which might have cramped his thinking later. Can a thing be done? The amateur does not know, so proceeds anyway. This is a kind of freedom that once known is hard to trade. And after his miserable upbringing, freedom must have meant everything to Pa.

•

In the town of Niederlahnstein on the banks of the Rhine, the family ran a drapery business. As the eldest of eleven children, Pa was expected to help his mother in the shop before and after school, and often long into the night: the shop stayed open until 11 pm. Mornings and evenings he also looked after the harnessing and stabling of his father's horse, kept for deliveries. Strict Catholics, they attended mass daily. Only at dusk on Sundays, after helping his father with unpacking goods and pricing, was he allowed out to play, running through the streets to find his mates who had been on the loose for hours.

On leaving school at fourteen, Pa pleaded with his father to let him become an engineer. He was sent to commercial school for a year instead to learn office and bookkeeping skills, which would be useful in future for the shop. He came top of the class. A job was found for him as a clerk in a factory office, but he was always in trouble for never being at his desk. Fascinated by the machinery and manufacturing processes, he haunted the factory floor. When not at work he was still expected to continue his shop duties. Small wonder he decided to run away. With a friend, he slipped off to the railway station one Sunday when everyone else was in church. In Luxembourg, then Paris, Pa's enterprising efforts to find a job came to nothing. In the City of Lights he was duped out of his belongings and the last of his money. After much privation, a charity helped him return home.

What to do with this wilful son? He implored his parents to let him work for an uncle who owned an engineering business. The perfect solution, you would think. Instead he was sent away to another uncle who was a baker. It's a move that seems deliberately mean, intended purely as punishment. As a grown man Pa was quietly spoken and warm-natured, with an impish sense of humour, and would have been so as a boy. Why would a parent wish to break such a child, who should have been a source of pride?

At the bakery in a town 200 kilometres from home, Pa's ten-hour day started just after midnight. He finished at lunchtime but before going to bed made the dough and rebuilt the fire in the oven for the next night's baking. On Sunday mornings they only worked for four hours, but then there was church, after which he was required to follow his uncle into town to watch him play billiards.

Pa was a male Cinderella. But there was no fairy godmother. He had to rescue himself.

After six months of saving money from his small wage, Pa had enough to decamp again, this time to Rotterdam, where the mistimed stowaway incident took place. Two years of working as a sailor followed, aboard tramp ships, oil tankers and even a three-masted sailing ship. He was trying to gain the experience necessary to become a ship's officer and possibly a captain; but his service on the sailing ship nearly did him in.

•

When I was ten or eleven I had a craze for reading sea stories: *Billy Budd*, *Two Years Before the Mast*, that sort of thing. I don't think it was because of Pa. I don't remember knowing much about his sea years when I was a kid, and anyway, I couldn't connect him, a real person I knew, to such a last-century form of transport. But those novels stayed with me, and I have a pretty good picture now of the conditions he must have endured. In his birthday speech, Pa gives a matter-of-fact account of the incident which almost cost him his life. During a blow at night he was assigned the main mast. Sent up to reef in the topsail, he stood on a swinging rope attached to the yardarm. The mast,

50 metres high, pitched in a wide arc while he tried to gather in sail with one hand and hang on with the other. Lightning strikes helped him to see what he was doing. A rope he was pulling on unexpectedly slackened and he was thrown off balance. For a moment he felt himself weightless, without a chance in the world of saving himself from falling to the deck below, but just at that instant the ship dived forward into a trough and he was reunited with the yardarm.

A change of career was necessary. At an English dock he found working passage on a migrant ship headed for Australia. Disembarking in Sydney, he was at last in charge of himself.

The year was 1912. He was nineteen years old.

•

Despite his early hardships, Ferdinand Hastrich (aka Pa) retained his sunny manner. In short time he found the local German community and got himself a job with a German wire-maker. A year later he was married. The following year he was naturalised as an Australian citizen.

With no English and no experience, his first job was to build a tennis court fence. Someone showed him how to cut and thread a pipe and left him to it. The fence stood for more than twenty years. As the wire business grew, Pa started making wire-working machines to improve processes for his employer. A job at a lift factory followed, then a job with a panel beater. The panel beater won a contract to make car bodies to fit imported Buick chassis, buying one of the new oxy welding plants to get the job done. It was the latest technology—so new, nobody knew how to use it, including the bloke sent to train them. Pa taught himself, welding the pieces of the 50 cars together with the care of a tailor. His skill became known to a large architectural metalworking company and he was poached to set up their welding section. There he remained until 1920. Then, as a 28 year old, he went out on his own.

•

The day Pa opened the Oxweld Co. on Parramatta Road was a dream come true. Two weeks later he blew the place up. He used an oxy cutter on an old drum he did not know had once stored petrol: the resultant explosion threw him on his back, and his dropped oxy torch set fire to what remained of the workshop. People came running out of the bank and the post office across the road.

Ever the optimist, he was not defeated. With the financial help of his brother-in-law he built a new workshop next door. From his drapery days, he fancied himself as a ticket- and sign-writer. But something of the heavy Gothic script he grew up with entered his written English, and his lettering always looked overworked and clumsy. He didn't notice. He was proud of his signs. On the big double doors facing Parramatta Road he set to work, painting a big red heart, split by a jagged crack running through it, and the slogan: *We Weld Anything but a Broken Heart.* Thereafter the business was locally known as the Broken Heart Welding Shop: it was a landmark.

A golden period followed for Pa. People took him at his word and brought him impossible jobs, the ones no one else would touch. A surgeon came with an instrument used for removing adenoids. The damaged part was finer than any welding wire Pa had to fix it, but the repair was done.

Pa loved tricks and puns so always enjoyed telling the story of fixing the statue of King Edward VII. The monarch, mounted on a horse, was prominently situated outside the Conservatorium of Music. (He has since been moved to a nearby traffic island.) The statue was not long installed when an embarrassing defect became apparent. The statue leaked. Every time it rained, water entered the statue via a crack in the base of the king's head, which was not welded but only screwed to the body. The belly of the horse filled with water. While it rained nobody noticed anything amiss. But when the rain stopped, the water inside continued to come out a drain hole located in just the right place for the king's horse to look like it was merrily pissing. The wee was rust-coloured, thus further drawing attention to the spectacle. For the boys and girls from the Conservatorium it was a great joke.

Pa told the government architect it would be impossible to weld the 4-hundredweight head in the cold air, but called for a long ladder to inspect the problem close up.

An agreement was reached. If the architect would erect a scaffold and wrap it in canvas to keep the cold out and the warmth in, Pa would take on the work. When the head was removed as a necessary part of the job, Pa took out the rusty iron bars he found inside the horse, and in their stead left his business card. Presumably it remains there: *Ferd Hastrich, Welder*. He could have added a new qualification: *Equine Urologist*.

In another 'art job', as he termed them, Pa was approached by a sculptor commissioned to make a bronze statue for the Leichhardt Council's war memorial. The artist had designed a 2-metre-high classical figure of a woman holding aloft the wreath of peace, but no foundry in Australia could cast it whole. The artist, seeing Pa's Broken Heart sign, wondered if Pa could make good on his boast. Suppose the statue was moulded in pieces, could Pa put them together?

Thirty-six separate parts of the woman—Peace—were duly cast, but as they cooled they shrank at different rates according to their various shapes. The artist was devastated. Pa's job was now inordinately harder, but he called for an extra hundred-weight of bronze rods and proceeded, filling here and cutting there. It was painstaking work to make the woman whole and the joins undetectable.

I have a copy of the page which documents the job in his scrapbook. There's a photo of the pieces as they were first given to him, arranged approximately but placed apart against a dark cloth background. The photo is, of course, black and white, but it is also much worn: scuffed and creased as if folded in a wallet for many years. This textures and flecks the mono-chrome, contributing a ghostly aura. The dismembered body, some parts whole, some parts halved, is spellbinding. The two profiles of the head face each other. A severed hand floats in the air. A bent arm, minus shoulder and wrist, emerges from the cloth. Breasts and bodice are split. The skirt of the gown is in shards. At the bottom, two feet point unnaturally down, as if with tendons cut.

The relationships between the parts are still there—the black cloth areas between them somehow hold them together, even while highlighting what's missing. Integration and dis-integration are in tension. The off-centre fold mark in the photo performs an extra dissection to the already dismembered body, isolating the slices of head in one panel.

I stare and stare. The photo is a simpler, haunting precursor of

Picasso's *Guernica*, perhaps the most famous anti-war painting in the world.

Honour to the dead, says the inscription on the plinth under the finished statue, shown in another picture. The completed woman looks uninvolved. As if she is doing her public duty but has to shut out her own wearying problems going on at home. Her raised forearm looks too thick. Whether that's Pa's fault or the sculptor's is unknown. Its chunkiness makes the wreath of peace that she holds look disproportionately small and almost toy-like, as if no one is expected to believe it.

On the same scrapbook page there's a photo of Pa, looking somewhat deranged. He's in his workshop, though most of it is in shadow. He's dressed in a white shirt and dark tie, and a black waistcoat with a fob chain. He's young and slim, has deep-set eyes and a smooth continental complexion. Perched high on his forehead is a pair of welding goggles; their round glass lenses catch the light. He's standing behind a waist-high collection of ironmongery: a metal frame, an engine block, bits of pipe and other miscellany. Low down, the face of a goggled co-worker pokes out of the junk. He must be lying on the floor or crouched low, because the position of his head is comically surprising, like the final reveal of a magic trick. Presumably all the gathered items are things they have cleverly fixed. Between them, Pa holds up a hastily handwritten sign bearing the Broken Heart Welding Shop symbol and slogan.

The photo is amusing—they have had fun in its impromptu staging—but in its scrapbook proximity to the unassembled woman it's disconcerting. The photos talk to each other, making Pa look like a criminally casual Dr Frankenstein.

It took Pa a long time to weld Peace together. It was slow and difficult, and because it had to be fitted in around his regular work, it could only be done at night. After expressing concern about delays, the mayor was invited by the artist to inspect progress.

'What countryman is the welder?' asked the mayor as they were leaving.

'French,' said the artist.

'Yes,' said the mayor. 'The French are clever people.'

It would not have done to reveal the welder's origins.

•

Recently, I went to visit Peace for the first time. She stands on a high granite plinth in a park which was formerly a cemetery. The plinth is inscribed with over 540 names. Of that number, 350 belong to the Leichhardt men who served in World War I, the war the memorial was built for.

In the sun, perched on a kerb, I sat with Peace for a while, thinking of Pa, alone in the dark workshop, carefully putting her together. Did he grow fond of her during the many nights he spent with her? Honour to the dead, indeed. By then, 1922, he must have known one of his brothers had been killed in the war, that another had been injured and yet another interned as a prisoner of war. He must also have realised that if he'd been allowed to follow his vocation in Germany, he would surely have ended up working in one of the massively expanding industries supporting the German war effort. I picture the white-blue of his oxy torch in the dark and, coming from it, showers of sparks.

Peace has a narrow, mannish face. A circlet of laurel leaves flattens her 1920s bob. She no longer holds the wreath of peace aloft; it's gone missing. But she looks more resolute without it— her stout arm not dangling a prize, but raised in protest.

In Australia it's hard to be martial for long. Our country resists it. That day, while I was sitting there in the sun, a fat magpie flew down out of a royal blue sky to make a graceless landing on the top of Peace's head. The bird had a worm in its beak. Up there, with its feet on her bronze hair, it tilted and bowed into the wind. It was in no hurry to fly off.

•

Now Pa finally had his own business he was able to realise some of his own ideas—of which he had plenty. He had invented tools and improved processes for previous employers, but now he was a young family man his attention turned to the home front. He invented a flushing toilet cistern that was superior to and cheaper than any on the market (*Silent, Sanitary, Sure* was the advertising tagline), later patenting a dual-flush system decades ahead of its time. A poor licensing decision led to the first model flopping, and the second was a flush too far for the public. A cradle-pram was next, then a picnic tent which could be assembled in various configurations and neatly packed into a suitcase.

A new age of family leisure was dawning and it was one Pa embraced. The annual Hastrich holiday, taken down on the south coast with a gang of relatives and friends, was one of simple hedonism, with days spent swimming and fishing. There was only one thing missing—a boat.

Naturally, if you are Pa, you make one—one that is versatile enough to answer to every possible requirement and desire, albeit on a small scale. And just as naturally, if you are Pa, you make your boat out of metal. Hence the Collapsible Boat and Trailer, patented 1932.

Made of sheet metal, the 10-foot-long double-ended dinghy was constructed in two halves which could be 'folded', one on top of the other, for transport. In this mode it looked like half a peapod. To transport it, the pod was placed in a trailable cradle, whose metal struts doubled as oars when the thing operated as a boat. Fishing gear and holiday luggage could be stored inside the pod during transit.

In a blurred newspaper photograph of an early prototype hitched to a car, the thing looks like a futuristic coffin. Suitable for the interment of contaminated bodies. Perhaps Pa missed an opportunity to patent for this further use.

Once at the holiday destination, the wheelbarrow-like trailer could be unbolted from the car and pushed to the water's edge. Locked open, the little boat accommodated five people. Airtight compartments made it unsinkable. A motor could be fitted to the stern or it could be rowed, but it could also be sailed. The canvas cover of the trailer converted to a sail when rigged to a mast erected from one of the oars. The second oar could be employed as a rudder. An ingenious improvement in a later drawing shows a solid trailer-wheel doubling to fulfil this role when attached into a special bracket. This attachment does rather undermine the beauty and credibility of the vessel, however. Wheels and boats do not generally look well together, unless in a paddle steamer. But on the still waters of the lagoon behind the surf beach, the boat looks boatish enough to be serviceable, and in the few tiny box Brownie photos I have, the occupants look as pleased as Punch.

In one picture three little boys are in the boat with Pa. The singleted one with the stickie-outie ears nearest him might be my dad. Of the other two, one might be my dad's younger brother; the other is probably a cousin. Neither of them could be Pa's oldest son, who by this time has been in an asylum for several years.

In these tiny photos everyone looks so happy; but the freest, most creative phase of Pa's life was rapidly coming to an end. The Great Depression tightened its grip and the Broken Heart Welding Shop closed. For the next twenty years Pa worked as the manager of a fertiliser factory in Glebe.

It was, quite literally, a shit job.

•

In the 1950s, after another war, the amateur engineer in Pa could be suppressed no more and he opened a workshop in the backyard of his Croydon home, manufacturing his own inventions. *Hastrich & Co.*, read the letterhead, *Manufacturers of Technical Novelties*. He made garden hose holders for watering the lawn; special coathangers for drip-dry garments; and windshields which fitted to the driver's-side window of cars. The shields stopped air from blasting into moving vehicles when the window was open, thereby saving the hairdos of passengers. Pa also made metal trays which sat stably on a person's lap for that newest of phenomena—the TV dinner. Another version, the Kartray, was designed to hold snacks at the drive-in. The Barbecue Mate, also known as Spike-M, was a skewering system whereby multiple meats could be turned at once—so labour-saving. I get the impression Pa couldn't bear standing around for too long, either to hold a hose or turn a chop.

All around the house there were other inventions not viable on a commercial scale—the automatic cat-feeding device, for example, which ensured his beloved animal would be fed on time whenever he was out playing cards. I remember a sliding door which mysteriously closed all by itself, thanks to a strung-up counterweight. And then, of course, there was his toilet cistern, which had been in operation for years. This was attached high up on the wall. A straggle of levers poked out the top, making childhood visits to the loo an unsettling experience. I always half suspected the toilet was an ejector seat, which might at any moment blast off.

We kids never snooped around or pried into cupboards, but would have loved to. After all, this was the home of a guy who once turned up at a fancy dress party in a dinner suit and bowler hat—quite a conservative outfit . . . until he pressed a button in his pocket and a cuckoo bird popped out of a door in his hat.

In the garden there were other idiosyncrasies I saw in no one else's yard: little wire cages around the carnations to make them grow straight; a set of swinging bar doors on the fenced-off vegetable garden; lines of beer bottles pushed into the ground to serve as edges of flower beds; metal pipes everywhere, bent and joined as trellises.

The backyard factory was in truth a couple of mismatched sheds with the walls between them knocked out to join them together in higgledy-piggledy fashion. Inside, the atmosphere was cave-like. Narrow walkways of slatted wooden flooring threaded between benches and shelves. Everywhere, absolutely everywhere, there were tools, many of Pa's own design. Pa had one or two employees, and family members sometimes worked for him too, but in the jumble of stuff it was impossible to know what anyone did. I remember the surprise I got when I once saw one of Pa's hose holders for sale at a Woolworths variety store. So it was true: Pa really did make things that ended up in real shops; they weren't just bits of bent wire covered in plastic that we had lying around the house. I felt proud. They were bits of bent wire in Woolies.

Some of Pa's inventions had serious industrial applications: a rotary metal hole punch; a self-levelling mechanism for extension ladders; improvements to the design of concrete re-inforcing; a sheet-metal bending machine. This last, patented just before he died aged 81, was to have been the biggie. A tool for the world.

•

While I'm partial to trying Heath Robinson fixes around the house and show a certain nascent aptitude for innovation in the manual arts, it's really not my strong suit. What I share with Pa is his spirit. It's the blind adventurousness of the amateur that allowed me to dare to write. Like him I have learnt my skills by trial and error; like him I have limited materials to hand; like him I counter deficits with what are sometimes ingenious, sometimes inelegant, workarounds. Under these circumstances I realise my overoptimistic visions with varying degrees of success. There is a certain naivety to that optimism which is a weakness and also a strength. It's an optimism that's aligned with zealotry and utopianism: it lights up us amateurs and gets us cracking, but it also means disappointments are felt extremely.

I think of Pa and his folding boat and I know exactly how it would have been, how charged he'd have been, excited in advance by all the fun that would fill it. He was not just making a boat, he was making the astonishment on the faces of his two younger sons and his nephews as the boat was assembled at the holiday place, the full genius of its versatility finally revealed. He was making all the fish they would catch in it, the fooling around with sail and oars. With that little vessel, he was making days of happiness for others, and he could already see them all.

But then I think of him sitting in it and I remember his other son. This child, Carl, was mentally disabled. A difficult birth was blamed, but Carl also suffered from uncontrolled epilepsy, so his condition worsened. By the time he was twelve his care was too much for Pa and Ma to manage at home. He was admitted to an adult institution on Peat Island on the Hawkesbury River, where he resided until he died, aged 32. His medical records are brutally brief: *Cannot give an account of himself.* The diagnosis was imbecility.

Pa obeyed the protocol when he wished to make the long trip to visit, sending respectful letters to the superintendent asking permission. But sometimes he must have burned to bypass that barrier and sail his wacky boat to the island, if not to rescue his son, then at least to give him a ride.

Of course, there was no rescue for Carl. No fix for his condition. For Pa, who so prized his intellectual freedom in his youth, it must have been especially bitter to know his boy was so alone, without the company—the hope and transporting solace—afforded by coherent thought.

Sometimes, on holidays down the south coast, sitting in that little boat without one of his sons must have been unbearable for Pa.

Inevitably, the amateur breaks their own heart. Reality will always come to blow out the candle of the ideal.

•

When I looked at Pa's scrapbook a few months ago it was the photo of Peace unassembled that struck me most, I suppose because I'd never paid much attention to it before. I was due to meet two writer friends for lunch the next day and thought I might use the opportunity to propose a shared project, one which we might do as an enjoyable exercise to stretch our writers' minds, with no intention of its ever going anywhere. I wanted us to try plotting a screenplay together—just the basic structure and an outline of scenes. I thought how good and loosening it would be to spend a day or so on it, carelessly chucking around ideas.

The hard thing would be coming up with a basic set-up with enough scope and interest in it to get us going; but that evening, the evening before the lunch, an idea jumped into my head that answered perfectly.

It could be a modern-day Frankenstein story. Bits of an unassembled statue are found and given to an artist to put together. Somehow the statue comes to life, but not healthily so. It's just sort of gaspingly alive and in pain. For some reason the artist has to hide it. It could go through stages of improvement and relapse when it was capable of some action, good and bad. Underneath, like Mary Shelley's original story, it would be about the ethical questions of bringing life into the world, quality of life and the right to death. In part, it would also be about the creation of art and the moral responsibilities involved. Thematically it could operate on these interesting levels behind the scenes, but still be a thrilling, modern monster movie on the surface.

Yes, I thought. That's excellent! That will serve very well. My friends will love it.

I felt jaunty as I went off to lunch.

Coincidentally, we were due to meet in the cafe at the Art Gallery of New South Wales.

Our usual form was to talk almost entirely about books and writing, but early on the conversation veered away to the personal and it was only right towards the end, when we were finishing up, that there was a chance to put my proposal. Lucinda and Charlotte were already mentally departing as I spoke and showed no interest in the idea of a plotting exercise. But when I pushed on to quickly relate a little of the scenario, Lucinda's eyes immediately filled with tears. 'Oh, but don't you see? This is you. This is your thing.'

She meant my failed novel. The one I'd had to put away because it was too ambitious and strange to come together. The one I still loved, and would do anything to revive.

Straightaway I agreed. It was, of course it was, I knew it.

Charlotte was gathering her things.

But in truth I hadn't seen it in those terms: me struggling to bring my own poorly formed artwork into the world, my artwork that could not properly live.

We kissed goodbye and Charlotte and Lu bustled off up the escalator together.

I went into the toilets and bawled.

•

There used to be a saying in Australia: 'Have a go, ya mug.' The amateur is the perennial mug, but doesn't need to be told: they apply themselves to their missions willingly, because their missions are truly their own. Behind the wonkiness of the amateur hides the purist, the non-conformist, the wilful soul. Amateurs are independent and unreasonably hopeful against the odds—that's their job.

At his eightieth birthday party Pa was a happy man, giving thanks to his wife and family. Winding up his speech, and no doubt surveying the roomful of relatives and friends, he said, 'And the ones that are satisfied I came into their life can drink with me the health of the man in the moon.'

Then, quoting a popular quiz show of the day, he delivered his final line. 'Thanks for listening, customers!'

As with many migrants, Pa's inexpert use of English no doubt made him seem less sophisticated than he really was. But that playful quality in him was real, and it's an important part of adventurous thinking.

To own a hat with a door in it is no bad thing. It makes up for the broken hearts.

The Boat Show

The gods always smile on the Sydney Boat Show. As they should. I've never been to one yet when it hasn't been sunny.

This year the whole thing seemed particularly good—and amusing. This was because I freshly saw how the show is really an umbrella for sheltering different tribes of boat lovers, each with their own aesthetic. Perhaps this was more apparent because I happened to see extreme examples of the various boatie types in the crowd. Or maybe, as capitalism wades deeper into its decadent phase, it's because the products that earmark each group have become notably more excessive, pursuing whatever it is they say or do to newly shameless levels. Probably it was a combination of both.

The morning I went was crisp and blue, but strong winds were forecast for the afternoon so I started outside at the floating display on the water at Darling Harbour. Cheek by jowl every year, the luxury boats are moored here in a complex system of pens especially installed for the occasion. In the past, there were always a few vessels in this area that the average Joe could almost afford, if he was madly keen and willing to clean out the family accounts. Not anymore. The wealth was astonishing—at every level of manufacture. In the stainless steel a new kind of shinier shine seemed to have been invented, and in the paint jobs there was a new viscosity to the colour—it could have been scooped out of the hulls in creamy dollops if someone handed out spoons. It was amazing that even this detailing seemed so richly improved in the space of twelve months.

When it came to boat styles, the old-money traditional look was just about gone. The design aesthetic replacing it was all modern European schmick: new shapes and hard edges; changed profiles which looked at once high-tech and as if a schoolboy drew up the first sketches, his pencil over-earnest on some of the outlines. And there weren't so many mini-ships— the luxury floating mansions fit for Gold Coast developers; they used to be the big drawcard for oohing-and-aahing plebs. Instead, there were mostly small- to medium-sized boats which cost just as much.

Modern iterations of open launches were popular. They referenced the classic James Bond style of Italian speedboat, and so contained only the essentials: a steering wheel, white botox-injected lounges, and dinky compartments which flipped open to become mirrored drinks cabinets. The appointments are necessarily limited, because the remaining two-thirds of such a boat must be given over to housing an engine which could power a ballistic missile.

On the floating docks there were many natty sales tents, client bars and outdoor rooms. These were manned by a new species of human. The males, all in their mid-thirties, had sunned, clean-shaven faces and short haircuts, just done. They wore tan chinos and tight white shirts with blue jackets. The women were younger but otherwise matched. Actors in a nautical *Truman Show*.

In the midst of these glam hospitality tents was one boat that particularly captured my attention—the Iguana. It offered a major practical advantage over all others. It was amphibious. And like its namesake, it was beautifully ugly. Parked on the dock, it stood on four legs joined to caterpillar tracks (like those on a tank or bulldozer). At 29 foot long, it was a lot of boat when high and dry out of the water. The promotional video playing on a nearby TV showed one of the super race at the helm, driving it up a Dubai beach towards a massive onion-domed palace. I could easily picture myself in it up the coast, rumbling down our street to the shore and rolling on triumphantly over the mudflats into the bay. Once afloat, the legs neatly retract at the push of a button until the hull assumes a more orthodox shape—though naturally one that's still very uber. The video didn't linger long on the land-traversing stage, and what shots there were tended to cut off the legs. No doubt this was to downplay the environmental degradation caused by the Iguana, as it merrily rips up fragile ecologies under its tracks. Also, the bloke driving it looked like a dick, standing in a boat on stilts. That wouldn't worry me though. I wouldn't care how I looked. Mindful of launching it in a more responsible manner, I could drive it all the way to the boat ramp at Pretty Beach, stopping on the way for bait at Gary's shop. Plus, with such a versatile vessel, I could start thinking laterally about how I used it. Instead of going straight home after fishing I could sail over to Woy Woy and walk the Iguana out of the water. Go on into town. Go straight through the doors of Deepwater Plaza and then into Coles. I could do the weekly grocery shop, literally cruising down the aisles. No trouble getting things off the top shelves.

All possible for only $760,000.

But that's without options. Not as seen. Everybody knows you've always got to option up.

•

The outdoor section was all very good, but the real interest of the boat show always lies inside, in the exhibition halls. There the aspirational suburbanites like me wander, each of us gravitating towards boats which best fit our budgets, and our obsessive preferences and desires.

There's always a water sports/leisure area where the wackier models tend to be, highly portable craft for those who don't have the space, or the means, for a boat and trailer, but are desperate to get out onto the water. It's guaranteed someone will be there proselytising a brand-new way of propulsion, which nevertheless looks old-fashioned—like Leonardo already thought of it, or my grandfather. This year it was a large surfboard contraption that could be wheeled to the shore and deployed. The user, grasping a tall set of handlebars like those on a child's scooter, steps up and down on pedals. Then, under the water, two little flaps move backwards and forwards like goldfish fins.

But my favourite innovation this year was the round boat. With a diameter of 2 metres, it's essentially a stable plastic disc, to which a mini electric motor can be attached. From a swivelling bicycle seat in the middle, the solo fisherman can reach everything: the handy hatches concealed in the floor; the cleverly placed drink holders. All very fine. But who among us yearns to be master of a grey doughnut?

Serious fishos (vile term) bypass all that kiddie nonsense and head to boats that are built like trucks. Mostly all New Zealand made, they're unbreakable. They look highly industrial, with chequer plate floors and unpainted aluminium hulls; any decorative touches are black or visi-vest orange. It's brute boating. Everything is well thought through and everything works. Top quality. Over-engineered to the point of hubris. It's my habit to linger among them for a while, because I admire their devotion to practicality, and in these days of pumped-out shoddiness I appreciate a well-made thing. But in the end the aesthetic is too much. There's an efficiency ethic here that runs to rapaciousness; an industrialism that borders on the martial. I just want to go out on the water, not to war.

As usual, retailers flogging big-brand tinnies and family boats had loads of models on show, all of which can be customised in endless ways. Yet it's impossible to find one that ticks every box on my dream boat list. But I already knew this would be the case. It's part of the fun. Not just for me, but for everyone here. As you walk around, you hear people saying stuff like, 'Not bad, but it's not beamy enough, and there's no anchor well.'

Human beings are funny about organising small spaces. And when the space is inherently unstable—i.e. a boat—they get even more hung up on functionality and the perfect layout, on the need for cubbyholes and gadgets to keep everything in place. (I suspect that, deep down, this goes beyond mere tidiness. It could be a manifestation of the god-like desire in many of us to create mini-worlds—models of perfection—over which it's possible to exercise absolute control.)

But it's actually important not to have all your requirements met in any one boat, because the tyre-kicking, the humming-and-hawing, the trading-off of priorities in pursuit of the nearest thing to perfection, are what make the dreaming fun. Probably much better fun than actual ownership.

For the dreaming to work, you have to enter into it seriously. You must pretend that, although you're in no rush, as soon as you see exactly the right one, you really will do the deal. What does this say about materialism? That the true pleasure is all in the dream. And if the boat show is anything to go by, the kind of dream you have says a lot about you.

So, I don't want a mainstream tinnie, or one of the high-end, imported American fibreglass boats—the kind that are advertised zooming around the Florida Keys: big centre consoles driven by rich teenagers. And I certainly don't want bogan bling, although I can never resist pausing for a while in its dazzling vicinity. This is the section where the ski and wakeboarding boats are parked. You can't help but smile at their mindless hedonism. This is where disco meets Batman. They are squat (their low centre of gravity helps them handle

tight turns), and made of fibreglass because it better absorbs
the slamming of high speeds. Plus, you can get better paint
jobs. It always looks like someone spilt glitter bottles here:
purples, lime green, pinks, slashes of silver. The hulls are
black underneath with fantastically twinkling sides. On the
specs posters, sound systems are listed first. Clearly the most
important thing.

Finally I found the boat I was hoping would be at the show.
The dealer's stand was out of the way and unmanned. Heaven.
I've had my eye on this boat as my new preferred option all year:
a Morningstar Bay Fisher 498F. Aluminium (made in Taiwan
and robot-welded), but said to ride like fibreglass. It has a sniff of
the truck-type about it with its practical set-up and no-nonsense
metal flooring; also, it comes with a lot of sensible extras on my
must-have list fitted as standard. But in all it has a much lighter
look and finish than the Kiwi boats, so only gestures towards
the heavy duty. The feature that at first seemed a treat and
is fast becoming highly desirable—if not a must-have—is the
swim platforms off the stern. They sit flush to the water on
either side of the motor, so it's easy to get in and out of the boat
if you go swimming. Or I could just sit there, legs dangling. So
although the boat is a lot bigger than my present tiny dinghy,
I could still get close to the water—helpful when bringing in
crabs; or, yeah, if I want to use my bathyscope. The Bay Fisher

is just over 16 foot long, with a centre console. Perfect for me to manage by myself and versatile enough that I can nudge in near mangroves, or go out on the ocean on a good day.

I've had the name picked out for years—the *Giant*. (The giant *Squid*.)

•

But for all that, do I really want a new boat? Can reality ever match imagined perfection? I have this fantasy that with a bigger boat I'll be out in the misty dawn, or in the summer dark with navigation lights switched on; that I'll explore every corner of the estuary in every season—that I'll live a watery life spending half my time out there, enriched, immeasurably, by everything I learn and see.

But will I? Will I really use the boat that much? I couldn't bear the guilt if not. Then again, if I don't give it a go, how will I know? Would I rather deny myself the opportunity of having a great lived experience for the sake of not taking a risk?

Of course, money tangles unattractively through all this; money is the risk. I have enough to buy a boat, especially if it was second-hand, but because I want to keep it at the marina, it's not a sensible use of finite resources. The annual marina fees are steep, and there are other ongoing costs in keeping a boat permanently on the water.

So the conundrum is deliciously poised. Just the idea of a future perfection, possible and almost in grasp, could be enough. I get genuine pleasure from my daydreaming, can quite often feel it physically releasing in me when I think about boats (or writing). Something to do with endorphins or dopamine, I suppose. To act on the daydream may only saddle me with disappointment if reality doesn't live up to expectations. And I know I would feel ashamed of badly wanting a material thing and then being dissatisfied, when I already have so much really, compared to so many others. A new, insufficiently loved vessel would be incontrovertible evidence of a moral failing. And the pleasure of the dream would forever be lost.

These days there's another consideration coming into the mix, and that's ageing. While my physical decline is not imminent (touch wood), the inevitability of it can't now be completely ignored—and that puts a further squeeze on any decision. Delayed gratification may mean no gratification. The golden future is shrinking.

I wonder why notions of ideal states, in whatever form they take, have always been so attractive to humankind. (The concept of heaven is as much about this as it is about ongoing existence.) Is it an evolutionary carrot built into us to keep us striving for something beyond our capabilities? Even so, isn't it weird that just the wanting delivers such strongly felt, such *real*, personal benefits in terms of pleasure? No doubt some psychologist or philosopher could explain all this in a minute.

But back to the boat show. Go along and watch the people and you will see it's all about the dream, the search for perfection in the face of inevitable compromise.

•

On leaving the exhibition halls, I called by the floating docks again for another quick look at the Iguana. Just to make sure I'd seen what I'd seen. By this time the wind was ripping through. Promotional banners and flags snapped like dogs at heels. It was the last day of the boat show—indeed, these were its last hours. The afternoon sun was bright but the wind was cold, the shadows growing. The super race grabbed at folding chairs skittering off and held their jackets close to their skinny bodies. Snap, snap. Soon, all the arrayed affluence would be packed up and sent back to wherever it came from.

On the bus on the way home I happily examined the few things I'd picked up: tide charts, two magazines and a couple of two-dollar packets of circle hooks. As the bus crossed the bridge, I glanced out the window. There, far beneath and stretching away, was the glittering path of Sydney Harbour.

149

Night Fishing

I.
ghosts

Still life. Items laid out on a cotton bedspread: the broken arm of a pair of spectacles, a watch, and a wallet, the notes spread out drying

•

Remember that day my father fell and we thought he was gone, or I did anyway, a chasm splitting in my chest as he disappeared into the water? The boat with all of us in it, my mother, sister, brother, me: the little clutch of us travelling on, leaving the spot where he disappeared.

We did not know how to stop the motor. And it was so loud it seemed no one could cry out or shout over the top of it, though perhaps we were struck dumb.

It had been hard to start. My father wound the leather strap around the flywheel of the old Blaxland engine and yanked again and again with such strenuous effort that no one talked; somehow to do so would be to belittle the commitment to each attempt. A glum mood settled as it increasingly seemed we would not be going anywhere. But just when my father's temper and the outing itself seemed exhausted, the motor powered to life and we set off.

It was autumn. The kind of autumn day of sharp outlines that presages winter with its quickly fading afternoons. We wore jumpers, and the water looked cold.

We had not gone far when it was somehow understood there was another problem: a newspaper parcel of bait remained on top of one of the wharf pylons. The boat could not be stopped in case the engine would not start again, and, for reasons I don't now recall, neither could it be set to idle. My father decided we would drive by and he would stand, one foot on the seat and one foot on the gunwale, to reach up and grab the bundle, while my mother, at the tiller, steered. He leant, indeed, almost stepped out in a Cartier-Bresson-caught moment with arm stretched, fingers spread ready to accept the shape of the parcel. And

152

that's when he disappeared between the boat and the wharf timbers armoured with oysters. In the boat, we left the circle of downthrust where he entered the water, and unstoppably motored on.

So many times we children had thrown rocks from the wharf, running backwards and forwards to the narrow, stone-strewn shoreline looking for the biggest we could carry and drop, studying with relish each plunge to oblivion.

My mother dragged on the tiller to head the boat back, but the arc of its turning circle was wide and slowly executed.

We twisted in our seats looking for him.

Finally, he reappeared.

While we motored in a holding pattern, Dad somehow hauled himself onto the lower landing of the wharf (bleeding at the temple from a red-running nick) and went on, up to the house to change into dry clothes. We were still frightened, we kids—not safe yet—and possibly my mother was nervous too, unaccustomed as she was to handling the boat. There was unspoken agreement that we needed to be quiet to let her concentrate, but she stayed outwardly calm and by example kept us somewhat reassured. When Dad returned she steered close and his leap back to us was executed without further trouble. I do not remember anything about the rest of the outing, except for seeing, on our return to the house, his things laid out on the bed in the front room. The image of that neat arrangement imprinted itself on my mind: the broken arm of his glasses; his watch; and his empty wallet, the notes spread out drying.

The wet money was especially troubling for its diminished power; something about its true nature revealed.

•

Fifteen years later, on a crisp, cloudless Saturday morning when I was 21, my father and I went out to play golf on a public course. When I got home, it was without him.

In the mid-afternoon of the same day I saw him again. This time I was with my mother and we were at Fremantle Hospital in the basement morgue.

Dad had died that morning in the middle of a dewy fairway still patterned with the footsteps of earlier players and the skidding tracks of balls. I had walked on ahead after hitting a shot and when I turned to see if he was close to catching up, he was where I'd last seen him, but lying flat on his back. I ran to him. A lit cigarette, still held in his fingers, was burning his hand. He made a few sounds, sighing exhalations, and I left him to go and get help. In retrospect this was a mistake, though not one I've blamed myself for. What I'd heard was agonal breathing, I later learnt. His heart had already stopped.

I ran to the clubhouse but at that early hour the doors were locked. I ran to the pro shop, passing people freshly arriving in their natty attire, but I was too stupidly shy and blank to simply stand still and call out for help.

The ambulance, when it finally came, lumbered across fairways.

By then, the dew had evaporated.

•

In the golf club car park I sat in the driver's seat of Dad's car. I had never driven an automatic. For a long time I sat there wondering if I could do it. I did not want to leave the car there; something made me feel responsible for getting it home. I suppose I had turned down offers of transport from the golf club staff, though I don't recall any now. It's only stop and go, I told myself. Only stop and go. People do it. And, very slowly, I drove the car home.

As I approached the front door, my mother came out with her handbag, smiling. She was just off to the shops to get us something for lunch. Looking past me for my father, she asked, not concerned, why we were home early, where was he? She was on the move, purposeful and happy on a sunny morning. I did not know how to start changing her day, her life. What I had to say would sound stupid. Like I was making it up.

•

Uncle Pete, the husband of one of my mother's sisters, drove us to the hospital. He was a GP and familiar with the place, able to escort us down backstairs and byways. In him, we had an insider as a guide, but our visit was official: we must identify the body, we'd been told. My father had died in a public place and this was the law. It didn't matter that I was with him at the time, although why it didn't matter, I never learnt.

In the basement corridor we stood waiting outside a closed door for somebody to arrive. The walls, I seem to remember, were painted skin-coloured pink, certainly not newly done.

I don't know now whether we were waiting a long time, but my mother and I were both struck with the need to go to the toilet and my uncle indicated a convenient bathroom down the hall. The bathroom was quiet, pink-tiled walls, the half-dozen stalls empty, doors open. We selected a cubicle each and began to urinate, and for each of us the stream leaving our bodies was so strong and powerful and went on so long—as if our organs and muscles had taken control to operate at peak efficiency to expel every drop of fluid from us—and it was so loud—as never-ending and as forceful as a horse's piss, destroying the bathroom's quiet—that we began to laugh. Emerging from the cubicles we continued laughing, the echoing sound of it ringing in the pink basement bathroom, genuine laughter, not hysterical. We could hardly stop ourselves, didn't want to, and we gave ourselves over to it and the enjoyment of it and it made us feel good. Two minutes later we were ushered through the door we had waited in front of previously.

The room was small, small like a storeroom, and in it my father lay on a trolley. A sheet was pulled up across his bare chest.

That seems odd to me now, why he needed to be naked so soon. What was the hurry? It was as if the staff had played dolls with him. It was their job, I can hear them explain, as if, years later, they are talking on a documentary film: 'It's just what you did. It's what you always did. They'd come in and you'd take off their clothes.'

Although that was the last time I saw him, I can't really recall how he looked. Reasonably normal, I think, as if greyly asleep. I remember my mother though, how she went to him and put her hand gently on his face, how she said in a small, miserable, wondering voice, 'He's so cold. He hated being cold.' As if really to say, how on earth did it come to this? As if this did after all prove him dead, for he would not willingly lie there. In her voice, too, was the bewildered acceptance that she could not fix it; there was nothing to be done to make him warm.

Next my uncle and the hospital attendant tried to remove Dad's wedding ring, but after a brief tussle they desisted, saying they would get it later. My uncle, who had years of experience in country practice, mentioned something about soap and string.

In another corridor, upstairs and lined with windows through which the continuing day flooded, Mum and I waited for the two young policemen who would eventually appear. There were papers to sign before we could go.

It was nice in the sun. By now perhaps we felt a little tired and not inclined to move; happy enough in our squares of sun. We had nothing to rush away to.

•

I think of Dad's death with equanimity now. This is how life is. Neither fair nor unfair. It just is. But I still miss him. And sometimes when I do, my throat tightens and my eyes sting, even after all this time.

In the dark night the red and green of the estuary's channel markers blink, pinpoints of light. On and off. Alternating pinpoints of light.

The time Dad fell in the water was unusual in that we were staying at the old holiday house by ourselves, without my parents' best friends, Pam and Clive and their children, whose house it was.

My father and Uncle Clive used to call each other Dad, fondly.

'Let's take the kids fishing.'

'Yes, Dad.'

And in the solid, broad-beamed old putt-putt boat, the two men took us.

The broken arm of his glasses on the bed, his watch, and his wallet, the notes spread out drying.

•

When my mother was taking her last breaths in the middle of the night twenty years after she was widowed, I was with her. And I said in the surest voice I could manage (though tension and urgency made it waver), 'Dad's there. He's waiting for you.'

I did not mean in heaven. I meant, in your imagination. I meant, make a picture of him in your head and go to him for comfort.

'He's there,' I told her.

This is what pictures are for. When we are help-less, this is what pictures are for.

II.

maiden voyage

I wanted to go, I said I'd go, so people were expecting me to go, there was a break in the weather, I went. Night fishing.

People said, Aren't you scared?

I wasn't scared, I knew what I was doing in daylight, knew where I was going inside out and back to front. Anyway, I had lights planned. Not proper lights, like on a proper boat (my boat is a little old beaten-up fibreglass dinghy), but lights as in a lantern, a torch and one of those miner's light things you can strap on your head if you don't care about your credibility. Okay, I was just a little bit scared, or, you might more accurately say, apprehensive. But not because of the woman thing, being a woman alone, which was, you could tell, what people were thinking. Although, okay, perhaps there was that too, just a little bit. Being alone out there in the dark with no one to help you if something goes wrong—well, the prospect of that could be just a little bit scary for anyone, if you let it. And then there was the man thing. Because what if blokes in their boat came near to me in mine? I would be just a bit apprehensive of what they might say, even though it's far more likely their behaviour would be friendly and not intimidating. But a woman meeting any man in the dark in, let's face it, an unusual situation is bound to invite comment and, well, it just is going to be an uncomfortable prospect, and that's a truth of the world.

But I choose not to entertain those thoughts. I can't let the idea of anything bad that's 99 per cent never going to happen stop me. Whenever I start to go wobbly when it comes to doing anything marine, I think of that kid, that sixteen-year-old girl who sailed around the world by herself, and I think, Jesus, don't be so pathetic. What I'm doing, where I'm going, it's nothing. I could swim home. And anyway, it's going to be beautiful and serene out there, it's going to be all Debussy.

So I'm going. For the first time ever in my life. Tonight. Night fishing. New moon, which means next to no moon, but this is my opportunity. It's cloudy, been sultry and rainy for days, so useful moonlight's out of the equation anyway. I had a rain jacket on but took it off. Too hot. I'm okay in shorts and a t-shirt, and the last time I looked the forecast said that the chance of showers was low—at last.

I load the gear into the dinghy slowly. No rush, waiting for the tide to rise. Set everything up in as organised a fashion as I can. Leave shore about 9.30 pm. Careful as I wade out with the boat, the water turbid and the various lights I've got at my disposal not greatly penetrating.

Almost straightaway a prawn materialises: translucent, elongated, zipping along on the surface and seemingly curious, swimming to the light, to me, with all the friendliness of a dog. As if wanting to lick my knees.

I wade quite a long way out to get past the part where it turns shallow again. In the narrow beam of the torch the water is cordial orange. No hope of seeing anything lying on the bottom before I tread on it.

Start the outboard, jump in, flip the motor into gear, I'm underway. And I look up into the middle of the bay and the new reality is immediately startling. I can't see. I'm going very slowly but my lantern, hanging on a pole shoved into a rod holder at the bow, is useless. It lights the interior of the boat well, but I also thought it would act as a brave standard, showing the way ahead, just like a London linkboy. In that moment I discover something obvious about the quality of different lights, forgotten in this indoor age. A lantern spills a pool of light but the focusing lens in a torch is needed to throw light forward, to make a beam that can seek out shapes and surfaces. The life of a linkboy would suck. No chance to see danger coming, only the snarl on its face when it arrives.

Where is everything? I'm motoring in the dark and, with a head explosion of what would be alarm if it wasn't counterweighted with disbelief, I think, Where are all the moored boats that I know to be there, where is the line of the oyster lease? I'm astonished. And for a moment the idea of going further, going night fishing, seems impossible. And stupid. This is why no one else is out here doing it. It can't be done. This is why there is only me. (Forget that it's a Tuesday, and the weather has been shitty for days, and how many people are in the habit of night fishing, anyway?) Why is the way ahead such a black hole when the sky is not dark but visibly filled with bulbous banks of aquatinted clouds, undercast with the light of town and distant suburb? It doesn't make sense. All around the bay, I can see house lights and streetlights, and can even discern the surrounding shapes of hills, but the water is a bowl of black.

After a moment of disorientation, I grab the torch and aim it out to where the boats should be, and at last the beam finds a yacht's red hull, rakes along it—dips into darkness—blue powerboat—darkness—sudden catamaran yellow: it's a Morse code in colour.

Swinging the beam to my right I find the reassuring white-painted tops of the posts of the lease-line. These sticks are my guiderail: keep the moored hulls all to my left, the sticks to my right, can't go wrong. Except this isn't all. Compounding my sensory overload while I'm trying to work everything out, all around me, in my sweeping light, things are jumping. Fish, prawns, I don't know what, leaping, flashing out of the water, skipping, chased, chasing, white-silver, all in such frivolous excess it's a baroque fountain of living things. The estuary spitting up its jewels. Here, there, left, right, my head's swivelling on my neck, where to look next? Every creature gone before it arrives.

Thank God for the extension wharf jutting out ahead. It's one stable thing I can aim for. There's something Van Gogh about the radiating municipal glow from the streetlight at the end of it; lonely and sterile, yet also reassuring, because it's there, at least it's there. That's what I think about the lights in Van Gogh's *Night Cafe*. The lamps hanging over the tables are beacons of despair, and yet real despair is no light at all. If something happens and I end up in the water, I can always swim back to the wharf and climb up the ladder that's recently been installed. A much better prospect than swimming to shore, swimming over weed and wading through weed, sinking in mud, stepping on unseen rocks studded with oysters; stepping, maybe, on a razor clam.

I'm motoring past the wharf and I'm judging the distance to where I want to be, which is in the channel between the wharf and the corner of the big lease. But where is the big lease? I seem far from the wharf and I should be seeing the sticks of the lease, but the sticks are spindles in the dark; is that the line, a further line or a close line? I seem far from the wharf, can't pause to look properly, the breeze is strong here, coming in gusts, turning the boat, I'm where?

There is the line.

I cut the motor and clamber for the anchor to get it out fast before I blow away in the dark. *Blow away?* I pay out rope, in the event; maybe not enough because later the boat swings like the hand on the dial of a crazy machine, lurching with every gust. I am bewildered by my circumstances—just a bit. Not out of control; it's more like I can never quite catch up to what's going on. It's only when I get a chance to settle that I realise the wind is an easterly, coming straight off the ocean over the top of the hill that cradles the estuary. The bottom of that hill was where I launched from. At the protected inner shore I couldn't feel the wind, couldn't *see* it, but it's biffing unimpeded out here. It's a while before I work out the gusts are coming in clusters with lulls in between. They don't seem indicative of steadily worsening weather. But it's still unnerving because I can't see further than the immediate surface of the water to definitively judge the safety of the situation. Or track how it might be changing. I have a new respect for those old seafarers who worked their craft across dark oceans in whatever weather: the physical danger of it, and the tricks of the mind. How did they all not go insane? I have heard it said sailors feared land more than sea and I understand that now too, having seen for myself the deception, the shapeshifting, how quickly things manifest and disappear. How easy it would be to run aground on shoals or rocks rearing up to ridicule maps.

The shore is not far away, perhaps 300 metres. By daylight I know it as a steep bush-covered hill with a single line of houses tucked high in the trees. Between me and the shore the windy water is a slurry of short post-impressionist brushstrokes going fast through a pathway of light, cast from a roadside streetlamp to the boat.

I start to fish. Put my two big handlines out, leaving them unattended, and begin with my rod as well. But then the big lines run, taking turns, and I have to lurch from one to the other to deal with them. Sometimes it's just the line getting dragged off the reel when the boat bucks as it swings on the anchor, but once definitely not, once with something strong on it pulling away. And I think, What are you, down there, and do I really want to know? What are you? The line seesaws, begins to cut into my hand, and I reach for a cloth to help hold it. I'm really going to need the cloth if this thing takes off. How will I manage if you're something big, something too big? And in my mind I see into the future to something coming up out of the murk, something large and rushing. It gets off. I'm glad. I'm also ashamed to be glad, so ready to do without the experience before I knew what the experience was. But I do not want to wrestle something big in the night, nor take something's life by accident if it's not a keeper, such a thing—a stingray or a small shark—being harder to handle in the dark. I do not want something to die for nothing.

After that I think, keep this simple: one big line out is enough. I don't really need to fish at all, except I said I was going night fishing so I need to be fishing. Otherwise this is just a fake outing, empty grandstanding. I thought this was going to be all Debussy, creatures gliding elegantly to me, not some ugly fight in the wind to the death. Keep it simple. A mistake could so easily be made, and alone here it could turn bad in ways daylight would never allow, that daylight would laugh at. Fishing is not the most important thing to do tonight. Look around.

And I do.

In the clouds there are torn holes showing patches of stars. Viewed this way, through tunnels of cloud, the stars seem all the more distant from earth, as if it's only ever by chance they allow themselves to be seen by us at all.

For days the clouds have been low-uddered with rain, brooding uncomfortably for hours, then, with no apparent provocation, spilling in heavy showers. I cannot tell if tonight's are any more or less threatening: the star patches open and close; the wind over the water seems a low animal. Nothing to do with movements above.

In the distance, the red and green blinking lights of the port and starboard channel markers are Christmassy pinpoints. Toggling off/on—the only sharp things in this thick humidity.

Gusts come and I wonder if it's foolish to stay, if this is building to something that won't abate. This is wind I would never normally fish in by day. But then the bullying is over for a few minutes and I think: I'm here now. Stay. This is what you came for, to be here, you're here, don't be frail. So I stay. But I think now that the anchor might not be holding. I seem closer to the sticks of the lease. Am I closer? On its tight rope the boat is perhaps bouncing the anchor free. I grab the torch and aim the beam: where? There? Yes, there are the sticks. They look closer. Are they closer? Soon I'll be over the weedy bottom that precedes them. Do it now, move now, don't wait until it's urgent, not in this wind.

I start the motor, I go forward to pull up the anchor, scurry back to the tiller, the boat spins. Which way am I facing? Where am I in relation to the light on the wharf? Another spin in another gust, the wharf's gone, there is the lease-line, is this far enough?

Hurried into my decision by the wind, I throw the anchor over and lean awkwardly around the lantern pole to tie the rope off. The lamp's LED white light fills the duck-egg blue dish of the boat but spills nowhere beyond. How it must look from above—from a helicopter, say: something sacred in the olive dark, the almost eye-shape of the hull filled with radiant blue-white. The imperfect fleck in it, me.

For a while I do not put out any fishing lines but sit in my glowing blue cup aiming the torch out into the dark water. Through the narrow column of light, individual straps of green ribbon weed pass in the current. They are vertically suspended, but upside down, so that the succulent white ends where they have pulled away from the plant's base ride nearest the surface. With their slightly curved-over heads, they look like Egyptian asps, risen up from the bottom. In imperious procession, on down their Nile they glide. And then a large, cobbled brown mass looms up from the cloudy deep—a lump of sargassum weed. It pulses, arms out like a ghost-train spook, before it fades back.

I return to fishing for a while, no bites; then finally get two small whiting which I give back. I do not in all truth want to catch anything. I reel in my lines. Take a last look at the boiling banks of sodium-infected clouds. A last look at the humped hill where the old holiday house of our childhood stood. Goodbye.

•

The way back is straight into the wind. The boat is so light, and so badly trimmed with my weight and the weight of the motor all in the rear, that the nose sticks right out of the water. I forgot my extension pole for the tiller. With it I can redress the balance by sitting on the middle seat to steer. I've forgotten it before, no big deal, I just drive along looking like the sort of rank fool I would myself scorn, but in this strong night wind, lifting and snatching, the hull's got no purchase on the black-mash of water. Gusts cuff across the bow, wresting the boat off course, and I tug and adjust. My sound mind says it's not that bad, nothing that can't be managed, while my unsound mind yelps, THIS IS MADNESS. Passing the wharf—the streetlight at the end broadcasts a cone of white light down over the main landing, a facility in waiting for a UFO.

Then, not long past the wharf, the land blocks the worst of the wind and crazed life suddenly flips again from the water in small explosions. I throttle back and put the motor into neutral to drift for a few minutes to watch. Blue fingerlings come close and become stationary, seeming to fall into a dream. A little red-eyed mantis shrimp skates into view. All around, things *plip* and *plash*. Mullet skip, a big one flashes by in an arc too fast to see but, like the cow jumping over the moon, it clears the boat, I swear.

That's enough. The tide is full, easiest to go the last part of the way home now while the water at the shore is deepest. That's enough. Some giant swordfish will be leaping next, twisting into the air, slashing arabesques with its swizzle-stick bill. Enough.

I pull in to the shore. Toss everything out of the boat onto the grassy bank. The breeze has now reached into this corner of the bay and the casuarinas respond. The sound through their needle leaves is a hollow note, sustained and choral, lifting and falling, wrapping around me and the boat and the street. A sound that's empty in the same way open arms are empty.

I am the only one out on this windy night. There's not a light on in any of the houses, no one, it seems, who can't sleep, who is reading, who is keeping company with a rerun on TV. This is my daytime dream, to have the entire place to myself. It's exhilarating. But it's also sobering, as if these people have turned their backs on me—this me—the strange wild thing out at midnight. I stand in the middle of the road. I have stepped out of the parallel universe of water and night and I could walk all these deserted streets, range far and wide around this model town. But they would not like to think of me out here if they knew. What are you doing? What could you possibly be doing? What sort of person, what sort of *woman*, is willingly out there in the wind, at night, alone? Delivered up from the estuary.

But what if I'm the one that's sane?

The salty air surges around me where I stand, bare feet splayed on the bitumen.

It's so powerful.
One spark in the combustible dark and the whole joint's
gonna blow.

III.
husband

In my first or second year of high school the idle talk among a group of girls one day revolved around the question, What sort of man will you marry?

When it was my turn to speak I had an honest answer ready, although how much I'd thought about the subject prior to the question being asked, I can't now say. But I was sure.

I would like to marry a fisherman, I said. The girls rolled their eyes and shrieked as one at such a choice, 'A fisherman!'

It hadn't occurred to me it might seem strange.

'Yes, but he would be a fisherman who loved reading.'

This the girls scorned, both as a possibility and as a redeeming quality.

I had not thought of my husband's work as low caste, or as barring him from books or learning, but if literature could not signal him as a man of worth and intelligence and thus elevate him, then clearly the wider world did not accord it the same importance I did. This was another shock.

But I could see it all. We would live in an isolated cottage by the sea. My husband would go out in his trawler at dawn and I would write. At night we would sit by an open fire and read books, classical music playing low in the background, perhaps. He had dark hair and a beard and wore roll-neck woollen jumpers (in all, bearing quite a strong resemblance to Mr Morrison, my primary school librarian). My husband was quietly spoken, thoughtful and strong, confident in himself and his capabilities. He often had a nice smile in his eyes when he looked at me. We would be equals in everything, except he would be more widely read than me (owing to the fact he was slightly older). He would bring other subjects and learning to me beyond the scope of my own interests, and I would never feel hemmed in by him.

Sometimes I would go out in the trawler with him and I would stand beside him at the helm, and although the deck might pitch as the boat bit into the swell (early-morning metallic blue; the odd gull riding the cold-edged breeze), we would be safe and all was exactly as it should be, heading for the fishing grounds.

Before I'd got much further than my husband's physical description, the girls laughed in chorus, so I cut the rest short.

'He'd stink!' they said.

'Would not,' I countered, hurt on his behalf.

'You couldn't want a fisherman!'

But I did.

•

Where have you been, my husband, my lover? Absent all these years.

Lost at sea.

Tonight, the ribbon weed asps have risen from the deep to tell the hard truth: 'It is we, instead of you, who have lain with him.'

The Nature of Words

Sometimes, in the recesses of the night when I can't sleep, I ask words to come to me. I give them a blank, black field to fly into. One at a time, I say in my head, whichever of you wishes, come forward.

For my part, I promise to do nothing. I don't want to rate them or otherwise judge, I don't want to join them together or mark them for future uses. I want only to look and listen to them in their plainest state, without any accompanying context.

When you have shown as much of yourselves as you wish, I tell them, you are free to go.

So they come, sometimes wanting to follow each other in a little trail of alliteration, but I discourage that. I want them at random. Unrelated. And absolutely unattached. Because it's their unadorned substance and character I want to appreciate, the entity each is unto itself.

Do painters do this too? Ask to be attended by colours?

apprehend
coo
parsimony
dolomite

Whether noun, verb or adjective, words are animated— by sound, definition, operation, rhythm, appearance or some combination of these. For example, coming out of the dark:

apprehend—
I like its measured air. Its meanings and the way they rock against each other: to catch, take into custody; and to understand.

coo—
Its compact simplicity and sound, inextricably bound up with the ancient impulse to soothe. Look at the way it's made: the shape of the 'c' an open mouth from which the 'oo' issues.

parsimony—
That long first syllable (at least the way I say it), sped up by the quick nimble rush of the rest. As if it regrets its duty to represent frugality and would rather have done with it.

dolomite—

Sharp edges, and the reliable heft of rock in its 'd'. I can almost feel a lump of it in my hand, begging to be chucked.

You see now how words have individual properties? Have active lives entwined with our own. Are more than mere signs. This is why they are fascinating to me and dear.

But if the words of my language are a precious part of my existence, how must others feel who have lost so many of theirs?

garawa	sea, ocean
wudal	rain, pour
gurumin	shadow of a person
mumaga	be lightning
warama	suckle, suck, feed (of a baby)
mudang	alive

These are words from the Darkinjung language group, one of the languages spoken on the New South Wales Central Coast and hinterland, collected as part of a language reclamation project. They're words I'd like to add to my lexicon, but they belong first to the families of their original speakers, who, for so long, have had to make do without them.

•

Maybe I invite words in in the middle of the night to make sure they're really all still there. Massed in their dark reservoir. Every word I ever heard, ever read. Maybe. Because some that come, surprise.

•

Words are company, comfort. And a means of escape. It was my mother who, by her example, taught me this. My parents weren't readers of books, but read the newspaper thoroughly each day. And Mum always did the crossword. The firm blue biro strokes of her block letters in the white squares demonstrated that thinking about words and sifting them were worthwhile. The right one mattered. Sometimes she would call out an easy clue but mostly it was a private, quiet pleasure, done at the kitchen table with a cup of tea.

In my mid-teens, when we were living in Melbourne, my dad lost his job in a recession. The family fortunes wobbled. Unable to find work, he bought a small business that made and sold billiard tables. It was the 1970s and the leisure industry was growing, but the downturn soon hit that sector too. Additional troubles followed.

Initially my mother worked two days a week in the showroom, which was distant from the workshop, but in short time she was needed Monday to Friday and Saturday mornings. She hated it. But she didn't complain, not wanting to make my father feel any worse than he already did. It was excruciatingly lonely and depressing. Sometimes the only time the shop door opened was to admit the postman bringing letters. When there was no mail, the door might not open at all. She spent her days behind a veneer partition which marked off a small office at the back of the shop. It was cheerless, with a concrete floor and spartan fittings. To occupy herself she sewed and, of course, did the crossword. By this stage my sister and brother had left home, so sometimes during the school holidays I'd go with her to keep her company, but it was hard to fill the hours. I read. We did the crossword together. We played Scrabble. In the showroom beyond the partition the different-sized billiard tables stood in ranks, as inert, and yet as pregnant with their future function, as coffins.

In the first weeks, when there was still cause for optimism, Mum came home one day laughing at herself. She told us that as she drove along Beach Road towards the shop, she was in the habit of glancing down the short side streets for snatched views of Port Phillip Bay. At a beach down one street, she noticed three swimmers. And they were there again the next time she drove by. In fact, every day, there they were. There was something robust and free about them that she admired, especially when it was windy and the waves were choppy and drab. The

179

way they turned up regardless. But that morning the realisation finally hit: the black, distant figures were actually the last remaining stumps of a derelict pier.

In the car on the way to work with her months later, I'd glance at those three stumps and hate them. Mum did not look. She didn't laugh at her mistake anymore.

Only once did she give voice to her despair. She told me that sometimes she felt like driving on and never coming back. It was a huge and frightening admission. She never said anything she didn't mean. What an enormous act of self-discipline and self-sacrifice it was to make the turn and pull in to the shop. She was so dignified about it, but now I imagine her, alone in the parked car, struggling to make herself get out, her head whirring with suppressed panic, wondering how she could manage another day.

I think words helped her. Her sewing was important too, but that mental reaching for words afforded a small window out to somewhere abstract and borderless. And at least with the cross-word she had the satisfaction of completing something in a day which otherwise might realise nothing.

Mum taught me a lot without seeming to, especially while we filled the Scrabble board together. Despite my wide reading, I was a poor speller. Look it up, she'd say. The dictionary was always at hand. It was a good one. If a customer arrived, disrupting our game, I'd browse its pages while Mum went out to serve. I loved that book, a big dictionary, bought through the post with a coupon cut from the newspaper.

The children's dictionaries we had for primary school, I always despised. Also the pocket Collins and Oxford hand-me-downs in high school, which kicked around in the bottom of my school-bag, inevitably with a shrivelled raisin stuck between the back pages, spilt from an ancient lunch. Those abbreviated volumes never worked properly. Half the time the word I wanted, or the word ending, was missing. And they were miserly, never giving anything more in their definitions than a bare boring minimum. But *The Age Encyclopaedic Dictionary* rarely let me down. And, astonishingly for that era, it also contained Australian words, and the names of Australian people and places. To see my own country's words included with the rest made me feel, not part of the world, but at least officially existing in parallel to it. In those pre-internet days, this was the family's only ready source of information. But, just like now, you could still find yourself going off on a little trail when you looked something up, pursuing terms mentioned or happened upon. The book was a way to travel. While Mum talked baize or slate or cue tips to a customer, I grazed over it, allowing curiosity to snag wherever it liked. Momentarily lifted somewhere else.

•

The words in Samuel Johnson's dictionary smell of the Thames and barrels of oysters and sprats. They have delightfully delinquent natures, so often bending away from the root of a word we're familiar with to audaciously couple with a stranger.

> muckender
> fleshquake
> eyeservant
> backfriend
> blinkard

When I visited Johnson's house in London a few years ago, I bought an abridged edition of his famous work, which was first published in 1755. I keep it within reach of my desk. At regular intervals I pick it up, not for Johnson's witty definitions, but for the energy of the words themselves, though I concede his blustering voice influences how I read. It doesn't matter that these are terms I'm unlikely to use. I dip here and there, and in the process feel my regard for all language refreshed. How amazing it is, that by these small building blocks we respond to our times, we create pictures, tell stories, bring form to the formless, make known the unknown, provoke feeling for the unfelt.

In the attic of his modest home, Dr J compiled his dictionary with the help of live-in assistants. Present-day visitors to the room encounter it largely unfurnished. Light from uncurtained dormer windows bathes the bare white walls, the wooden floors: it's an airy space, fit for all those words to bump about in. Around the heads of those long-dead dictionary workers, it's easy to picture them—nouns, adjectives, verbs—swooping and jostling for inclusion.

But it's what went on across town in Bloomsbury nearly a hundred years later that I really admire. There, a meticulous rationalist put together a dispassionate collection of words; one which shows itself on close inspection to be unexpectedly noble—and moving.

•

How can I make you fall in love with Peter Mark Roget's *Thesaurus*? Perhaps you would need to own a second-hand 1962 Longman's edition, as I do. You would need to sit next to me on the day when, after consulting it in my usual unthinking way, I idly wondered which word above all others Roget had chosen to be first.

Look. It is *esse*. Essential nature or essence.

So fundamentally apt it gives us both a little jolt.

Of course this is the word to start with. There could be no other.

The heading above is *Existence*; the heading over the next set of words is *Non-existence*. And that's when it dawns on us both (if you are ignorant like me and didn't know already) that an intelligent—even elegant—system of organisation must be in operation here. Together we immediately read the preliminary pages of the book, which include Roget's original introduction. We like the modest man we meet, as well as his grand design. For that's what Roget should really be famous for: not the idea of listing synonyms (in any case he wasn't the first to do it), but their beautiful arrangement.

Peter Mark Roget was born in London. His father was Swiss— hence the surname, which, as an Australian child of the suburbs, I've never felt entirely confident pronouncing. The year was 1779. Less than a decade before, Lieutenant James Cook had dropped the anchor of the *Endeavour* into the shallow waters of Botany Bay, an act which would eventually lead to the disruption and destruction of many of the continent's original languages.

This was the questing, collecting age which gave rise to modern science, and Roget was to take a significant place in it, presiding over its tail end. As a boy he was precociously bright, earning a medical degree from Edinburgh University by the age of nineteen. As an adult he was a renowned polymath, prac- tising as a physician, but active across all of Britain's leading scholarly societies, including the Royal Society of London for Improving Natural Knowledge, of which he was secretary for decades. He was busy. He lectured extensively on human and animal physiology; he wrote for the *Encyclopaedia Britannica* on a cornucopia of subjects; he invented the 'log-log' slide rule; he made observations on human optics which ultimately led to the development of cinema. These were just a few of his activities and achievements, and it wasn't until he finally retired, aged nearly 70, that he had the time to turn his mind to the word lists that became his *Thesaurus*.

As a young man preparing his first series of lectures for medical students, Roget felt his writing skills weren't up to scratch. He knew that clarity and precision of expression were crucial to communicating ideas successfully, but found, as he later said, that it wasn't always easy to summon the right word up from 'the vasty deep'. His remedy was to make lists of synonyms, grouped by subject, to help him select the most fitting word with just the right shade of meaning, tone and weight for the given task. Roget used these handy lists all his life, finding them indispensable, not just because they improved the style of his writing, but also because they helped him think. With words arranged 'not alphabetically, but according to ideas they express', he found that, by association, new trains of thought often came to him, prompting him to change tack or qualify his original position.

For three or four years Roget retreated to his townhouse (which was just off Russell Square—don't go looking for it, it's no longer there), adding words to his existing cache and marshalling them into a hierarchy of classes and divisions. His bent towards classification was not an original impulse, nor, as one over-egging biographer would have it, did it indicate an unduly obsessive nature. It was an interest of his age. The botanist Carl Linnaeus (who died the year before Roget was born) spent the last decades of his life developing the system of taxonomy that we still use today for the classification and naming of plants and animals. Roget was well aware of it, also of calls by a prominent moral philosopher, Dugald Stewart, for the principles of classification to be applied to abstract thought. Stewart believed the development of human knowledge had been held back because too little attention had been paid to language, the cornerstone of reasoning.

For the published *Thesaurus* Roget settled on six primary classes. Within the cool brackets of these half-dozen categories, words for all experience and living are collected, graded and apportioned:

Abstract Relations (including such things as Quantity,
    Time, Causation)
Space (including Motion, or change of place)
Matter
Intellect
Volition
Sentient and Moral Powers

Just as Linnaeus had done for the natural world, Roget gave shape to the amorphous chaos of human thought. With the delineations of these conceptual groups, the outlines of thinking were finally visible. And like Linnaeus's taxonomy, the beauty of Roget's system is that it's not closed: it admits change, accommodating new entries as human knowledge expands and experience evolves. Under its shelter there is potentially room for all the words that make the world.

I like to think of my *Roget's Thesaurus* as a construction—a kind of fantastic birdhouse for words, with many roofs and windows and open doorways; where no room is a dead end, even those in the innermost reaches; where the occupants might enter by one archway and leave by another; where everything interrelates.

Sometimes I think of the words that visit me in the night as birds, coming out briefly to stretch their wings, and of myself as a slightly wacky birder, observing from a hide.

•

When first published in 1852, Roget's 'birdhouse' sold at a persistent trickle; enough to warrant the reprints and revised editions that appeared regularly for the rest of his life. Amending the work became a family business, with Roget's son, then grandson, taking over. In 1913 the crossword puzzle was invented, appearing in the 'Fun' pages of the US weekend newspaper the *New York World*. Synonyms were suddenly in hot demand as the craze went global. The *Thesaurus* took off. It was by this means that the book found its way into so many English-speaking homes.

Most modern thesauri have been dumbed down. In UK publishing territories the name 'Roget' has been trademarked, but in the US it's a generic term for any book containing synonyms. Across thesaurus brands many different organising systems are employed. The majority have done away with conceptual groupings, relying on straightforward alphabetisation, which to my mind immediately reduces half the value of the book. Where classes are still used, headings tend to be dull and have lost the power to provoke, no longer hinting at anything grand or philosophical.

The magnificent achievement of the real *Roget's* is that words in one idea group are situated alongside opposite and correlative ideas. The set-up is useful for practical reasons, providing a browsing environment for deeper consideration of the word required, perhaps even prompting a flipping of the phrasing of a sentence in order to use a negative version. As Roget hoped, his thesaurus encourages more active, critical thinking during the process of writing. But the arrangement of related ideas is important for another reason: it makes for a poetic resonance which can inspire. Flick through the pages to do with sound, for example, and there you find headings ranging from *Silence* to *Loudness, Resonance* and *Non-resonance, Human Cry, Animal Sounds, Concord, Discord, Music, Musician, Hearing, Deafness.* You have sampled the multiplicity of all sounds on earth, and glimpsed their absence.

And *Existence* and *Non-existence,* those first two headings in my Longman's edition; what a simple pair of hands they are, holding out a mixed bag of profound complexity. In happening upon these entries we pause, momentarily reminded of the mighty notions which every day of our lives follow us like shadows.

•

Up the coast at the holiday house I keep a Penguin *Roget's* and a very decent *Macquarie Dictionary.* It's our custom to do the crossword communally, and if we remain stumped by the last one or two clues we consult them. The internet provides faster, pat answers, but it's ultimately unsatisfying. It's too quick, and the opportunity for ambling research and incidental discovery is lost. We're not as good at completing the crossword as Mum was, but as a holiday ritual it's a pleasant accompaniment to our days—out on the deck with coffee, later shoved into the beach bag to be further considered under the umbrella between swims.

When my sister comes to visit, the Scrabble board comes out, the same old family set Mum and I used at the shop all those years ago. Di and I sit together at the table in the long verandah room, usually in the late afternoon when the western sun hits the cane blinds. It's nice. We take turns to pull a tile out of the cloth drawstring bag that holds the letters, to see who'll go first. Our mum made that bag out of a scrap from the bedspread she sewed for my brother when he was little: broad emerald green and royal blue stripes, the material a very strong cotton.

I like the quiet concentration of those afternoons, the plastic click of the tiles against the wooden ledges as we shuffle the letters looking for words. Passing the heavy dictionary to each other from time to time. We play lots of ordinary words, but when an unusual one is laid out we make noises of appreciation. It doesn't have to be terribly exotic or clever to earn our admiration. It might just be one we haven't seen in a good while and didn't expect to turn up in these parts.

We play to win but not stupidly so, more in the spirit of staying sharp so that a loss is honourable and a win, even if you've been lucky with letters, has taken some effort of concentration, a proper engagement. Old notepads filled with scores show the wins evenly spread between us. One I kept for a while had Mum's scores on it from when the three of us were last all together. At a point I don't recall, just through the normal process of ageing, she stopped winning, missing words and places she could have played, would have played, in the past. I didn't like noticing that. Or when occasionally I saw her, a little exasperated, put her fingers to her temple to think, as if to press something more out of there.

The click of the tiles. The orphaned Q. The blank.

Words forming and unforming.

•

Maybe I invite words in in the middle of the night to test if they're really all still there, waiting and available. By day, when I'm writing, they are so often reluctant to come, refusing to line up in coherent strings. That's when I'm reduced. To yanking them down by the collar and nailing them to the page.

It's a bloody way to create a society, as any dictator will tell you. And afterwards, it takes a long time to clean up the mess.

•

The unreliability, the mutability of words as materials. And yet the right one occupies its place so solidly.

•

Recently I've been looking at the work of the visual artist Cy Twombly (1928–2011). That guy really knew how to paint words. He understood the movement in them and the way they can travel across time. He loved poetry and quoted it extensively in his art; the enduring potency of classical myths also fascinated him, and the names of gods and mythic figures often feature in his work.

As a young man Twombly served in the army as a cryptographer. Words appearing and disappearing must have infected his dreams. He paints them worn or scratched or faded or dripping—packed with resonant qualities. They are messages from another realm but meaning is always in process, struggling to form. Often words are not even whole: letters might be exploded, or a character might be repeated across the canvas in a scrawled flow, as if to represent the irrepressible, recurring lyric of prayer or song.

In their repeated struggle to manifest, I think Twombly's words enact the effort of successive generations to call out to the future. Perhaps they wish to say, We were here; perhaps they wish to say, Listen; perhaps they just want to say hello.

Through Cy Twombly's art I see very clearly that language operates at the threshold between order and chaos. It's on this step humans live. From that narrow place, all our lives, we look out, trying to make sense of it all.

Helping us manage this was Peter Mark Roget. By putting a structure around language—an architectural folly—he made visible life's manifold variegation, and showed us it need not be overwhelming.

•

In the past couple of years there's been a burst of projects aimed at maintaining and rehabilitating Australian Indigenous languages. A new optimism seems to be growing, with many participants finding the learning and sharing of language to be unexpectedly strengthening and powerful. To me, this makes perfect sense.

I often listen in to a current radio series which asks Aboriginal people from language groups right around the country to share a few of their favourite words. Who knows how old some of those words are—maybe 60,000 years or more—the oldest human words still spoken. Other words are recent; adaptive and clever. Some words describe concepts or activities for which there is no English equivalent, and so contain singular knowledge. But where there are equivalents, it's not just about replacing the labels on things. You can hear some of the properties inside the language words moving again, declaring their nature; and in the voices of the speakers, snatches of the present world starting to make a new coherence.

In one episode, a young man from Menindee in western New South Wales, Andrew Sloane, says that an important word for him is *ngamakuuluyi*. It's from Paakantyi language.

'That means *my dear mother*,' he says. 'Me and William have always said it after we found out his grandfather said it to his mother.'

Andrew explains that he lives with his grandparents and says it to his grandmother. An unstoppable warmth enters his voice here. 'They know what it means.'

The words of our country are stirring. To listen is also to be changed. The more that fly through the night the better. Room for plenty under the shelter of old Roget's *Thesaurus*.

esse
mudang

My mother, pressing her hand to her temple.

Coming out of the dark

— continuum —

Time-stretched with its double 'u'.

The Butcher and the Housekeeper

When I get up in the morning and go into the kitchen of the house up the coast, I am mildly surprised to find it tidy. This is because I dreamt last night of a middle-aged couple breakfasting there. While everything is as I last left it, their recent presence is palpable.

The man, a butcher by trade, is doing the cooking: halved tomatoes, fried—which have caught on the bottom of the pan and blackened, but not unpalatably so. The woman, a housekeeper for a wealthy Belgian family, watches without criticism. Their faces are not well defined but there is a very sure sense of the way each of them occupies space physically: the butcher standing beside his pan on the stove, a big man, tall; the woman sitting on a stool, the grounded weight of her buttocks on the seat, her head cupped in a plump hand as she leans heavily on the island bench.

As is the way with dreams, the kitchen, which is my kitchen even though it doesn't look like my kitchen, is not my kitchen at all. It belongs to the Belgians, who are apparently away.

The butcher has been asking the housekeeper out for many months without the slightest indication of return interest on her part. Whenever she visits his shop he is playful (in a light, deft way, not in the clichéd manner of men of his trade); she is dour. He is comfortable with her refusals and expects nothing of her, but her directness intrigues him and his continuing invitations remain sincere.

One day, a day not dissimilar to any other, the woman capitulates, agreeing to an outing. The butcher is surprised but pleased. It is clear she has not weakened on the spur of the moment, but in fact seems to have come into the shop with her mind made up. There is nothing to say why she has made this decision, but there is no doubt it has been arrived at rationally, and with grave reluctance.

As proof of her premeditation we somehow know she has been to a beauty salon to get her (late) middle-aged body attended to: legs waxed to the line of her underpants, feet soaked and softened, calluses pared back, toenails cut (she refuses all offers of varnish and even clear lacquer). She has had these basics done to make nakedness possible. To do more to the body would have been to attempt a stupid lie, a lie she has no patience for.

All this she has done in a resigned, practical way, baring herself to the young beautician as one might to a doctor performing an invasive medical examination—deliberately not entering mentally into the details.

And the couple's outing? What was the nature of their outing? There is nothing to say what their outing was, but for certain it was short. The woman did not want to play getting-to-know-you in a restaurant, holding a glass of rosé. Perhaps they stayed in for a drink. Why not? They had the house to themselves; the Belgians are away.

In the kitchen the next morning, the butcher is cheerful as he tends the pan, spatula in hand. He has the interior energy and constancy of the optimist in him. She, of course, is a pessimist. He accepts her slumped posture at the bench and her frank observation of him without taking it as a comment. Her negative presence is just as strong as his positive, and it carries just as much life force.

•

When I enter the kitchen to make coffee they are not there. Clean benches. Almost sterile. And yet the strong sense they were lately here, the man at the stove, the woman on the stool. The pan with its red, red halves of tomatoes.

In my kitchen, while I slept, these people have been. And in the rippling disturbance they have left behind, I see and admire their mature courage.

•

For three years I have not written any fiction. My just-gone visitors make me realise how much I miss it. Though they were only here briefly, I liked them both a good deal.

All day the house feels nicely balanced, empty and full at the same time.

The History of Lawn Mowing

These days when I'm mowing the grassy knoll in front of the holiday house, I always think of the writer Georgia Blain. I didn't know Georgia personally, but friends of mine did. By their accounts, and Georgia's own, she loved the domestic chore of mowing.

I get it. The physical push and pull of it, the purposeful striding when there's a long straight stretch and the way the motor's ear-filling roar puts a bubble around you (although Georgia's mower was manual, so she didn't experience that bonus). There's the joy of the transformation wrought, the domestic space brought to order, made inviting, hospitable, comfortable, beautiful for those you love, as well as the world at large. And there's the undeniable satisfaction of completing a definable task, with discernible results, in a relatively short space of time. The great pleasure of this last should not be underestimated for a writer.

So I'm mowing and I'm thinking of Georgia, in a celebratory, sisterhood kind of way, even though it was in the midst of this act that Georgia was felled. In her backyard, on a vivid, good-humoured day of sunshine, she had a seizure. It was the unwanted herald of unwanted news: the first symptom of a brain tumour of the worst kind. Felled, smote, struck down. By sudden visitation, her life was changed.

While I'm mowing, I don't think about the months of awfulness and the steady losses that ensued for Georgia and her family, although I've read what she wrote about that time, and have an imagination I can use. Instead I deliberately keep it simple: I just mow for us both, in cheerful acknowledgement of that woman's sensible pleasure. And with respect for the sharpness of life; for the way, as Georgia's story demonstrates, life so often does that bittersweet thing of being fucked up and apt at the same time.

Georgia's companionship adds a new element to the job of mowing, but for me, here, it has never been a thoughtless task.

•

I keep the mower around the back, under the house. The house sits lengthways on the tiny block of land and there's a good dry waist-high space at the western end where the ground slopes away towards the place next door and the bay. The dirt under the house is grey/black and so dry it's almost dust. Years ago I put an old carpet there that we were going to throw out, and I park the mower on top of that. To retrieve the machine I crouch down and waddle in a little, past the brick pilings on which the house rests. As I shuffle in I kick more dust onto the carpet and always a couple of shells. Beyond the rectangle of carpet are more shells, hundreds of, thousands of shells and parts of shells: cockles, whelks and more cockles upon cockles; bleached by age, they white-fleck the dirt. Shells that must be, there in the topsoil, more than 200 years old. I do not know how deep they go or how far they extend. Mixed with them, here and there, and over there and there and there, are small pieces of broken asbestos sheeting. Ranging in size from a thumbnail to a saucer.

•

My elderly neighbours tell me the house was brought here on a barge. At least, that's the story they were told, in turn, by an old-timer. When might that have been? I ask, but they don't know for sure. Maybe the forties. When building materials were scarce because of the war. Everything was reused, repurposed, materials scavenged.

Almost every window in the place is different, so the dating makes sense.

When it sailed in, the house would probably have been just its core self: a little oblong wooden box, compartmentalised into three rooms of equal size, side by side, with a verandah running along the front and around each short end. Only afterwards would the verandahs have been closed in with fibro sheeting to make what are now the other rooms.

For many years, I believe, the house was used as a rough fishing shack, and perhaps went unattended or even abandoned for long periods. It may have been vandalised, the fibro bashed in then replaced. Easy to throw the broken asbestos pieces under the house. There to mix histories with the midden on which the house was set. There to wait and disintegrate into poison fibres.

•

When we holidayed in this area as kids we never knew anything of the Aboriginal people who lived here first. We knew of middens (rubbish tips, my dad said they were, but it was an engineer's cut-and-dried comment, recognition of the universal need for such an amenity, and left at that), and there was also hearsay of paintings in a cave in the bush, high up on the hill behind the old house we stayed in. (The cave was too far away for little legs to travel, I was told. I did not know where it was, and I never went.) But what seems astonishing today, in these comparatively enlightened times, is that the middens, the cave, were somehow completely disassociated from any actual people. And so it never occurred to me to think of Aboriginal men, women and children once walking the same tracks I walked, or fishing or watching the waterway as I was so fond of doing. Nor did I know of or wonder about those families' dispossession. I grew up in, was schooled in, that long era of deliberate and coordinated white forgetting.

Though I try to pick up whatever bits of information I can, specific, local knowledge about Indigenous life is more than ordinarily difficult to obtain, for good reason. The country of the Central Coast belongs to the Guringai and Darkinjung people, but the boundaries are unclear, and the names of the smaller groups who made their home here are unknown. The smallpox that the first colonisers brought with them quickly spread to this region from Sydney, devastating the population. The few survivors were isolated, their families and clan networks destroyed.

Settlers took over the land early, because it was easily accessible by boat, and most of the first people were gone. They set up subsistence farms, cut timber, and for decades dug out the most convenient middens, sending the shell to

Sydney for lime burning; lime to make the mortar which would build the city.

Rudimentary archaeological surveys carried out in the 1970s and 80s show what common sense should already have known—this little peninsula was resource rich and a favoured place of occupation for Aboriginal people. In these few square miles over 80 sites and middens have been logged. When I go walking now, I see evidence of the busy activity of Indigenous living everywhere. By the estuary, more middens (which we understand now as campsites where people prepared and ate food around cook fires, and where, on occasion, the dead were buried), while up on the ridgelines every rock platform is worth a second look for grinding grooves or engravings. Fire trails cut into the orange soils often have, exposed in their banked sides, patches of white clay suitable for painting body or cave.

Like Mungo Man rising from the ground to show himself, it seems the old people and the old ways are coming forward to instruct. When a recent spot fire swept through a section of bush at Box Head, a rock platform was revealed just off the track. On it were engravings of a boomerang and two decorated shields, also the pecked outline of a fish, just begun. Strong winds have since stripped the burnt leaves from the trees. They lie as litter, perhaps to be scattered back over the rock by the next blow, the process of covering beginning again, to keep the site safe for another generation.

On exposed plateaus some of the engravings are worn faint and almost away, but on one the firm outline of a kangaroo jumps strongly alive. From that platform both the coastline and the hinterland may be viewed: it is close to the sky. I can imagine how powerful it would be, to stand there in full possession of the encyclopaedic knowledge that belongs to that spot, to know all its songs and stories—stories in which law, land, food and culture are indivisible.

Wherever humans are, landscape is not long without culture. I was born in Australia, but to my interactions with the natural world I bring the Western tradition of art, and Western systems of knowledge. They're what I was given. And so Milton and Galileo and Van Gogh appear in my writing, to help me describe and make meaning from my estuary. They are an inadequate fit but I make the best of it. I say to that art, that thinking: *You're here in this country now, so come on. Bend yourselves to perform in local conditions. Come out of your cathedrals and museums and work for me here.*

But the great forgetting is lifting. Indigenous knowledge is beginning to be valued by non-Indigenous Australia, and, with enormous generosity, Aboriginal people have responded, sharing what is appropriate, to offer a glimpse of this country's greater inheritance and belonging.

Children will grow up knowing much more detail about their own country than I did. And always when there is knowing, something new can be made from it.

•

When I put the mower back under the house, the asbestos scraps I see there remind me of a visit I once paid to the matriarch of a settler family. She lived in a huge old mansion on the family spread in the Southern Highlands. I was to interview her for an article I was writing and she kindly invited me to stay the night so our conversation could extend.

As soon as I pulled up to the steps of the mansion in my old Toyota Camry, the front door opened and Janet popped out to greet me. She was nimble-bodied and, in smart, figure-hugging casuals, was youthfully dressed for her 80 years of age—and friendly. On the verandah she looked down and said, 'Oh, don't mind that, watch out,' and tapped her foot towards an enormous blob of bird shit. We proceeded inside to the hallway, down which I could have driven the Camry, with plenty of room either side.

First, we got my few things into the ground-floor bedroom I'd been allocated, and then we headed off to the kitchen—all at a kind of skip to cover the distances—while Janet kept up an absent-minded commentary. 'Can you smell something? The kids came up yesterday and said there was a smell. Must be a dead rat under the house somewhere, but they brought up the dogs and couldn't find anything.'

Indeed, there was a smell. It was especially putrid down the end of the kilometre-long hallway near the dining room, through which one had to go to access the homely kitchen, passing a mahogany table which could easily have accommodated twenty. As we travelled, the rat smell—like super-intensified dampness mixed with fertiliser—curled around the warrened corners of the house, absent in one room but unexpectedly reappearing in another.

'I haven't turned the central heating on,' said Janet. 'Don't want to spread it.'

Later, carrying a drinks tray into a sitting area under the complicated stairway in the baronial hall where there was an open fire, she said, 'Yes, I think there is something there.'

That there could be any doubt was a wonder to me. As she handed me a biscuit piled with smoked trout, I mildly agreed.

That night as I lay in bed I thought I could detect whiffs of it entering, hanging in layers in the air. I tried to school myself to think of something else. But then, perhaps, there was another whiff. Past the dark shapes in the room—the queen bed and the single bed, the divan, the big wardrobe and two dressing tables—in it crept, for sure. Those clammy whiffs, falling in slow motion, must be settling on my sheets. I thought of the clothes I'd left out hanging and the smell of death climbing in.

I could not sleep. I was Lockwood in his closet-bed in *Wuthering Heights*, suffering visions.

•

In the afternoon we had gone on a tour of the house—well, of most of the ground floor. I wasn't invited upstairs. Rooms led on to rooms. We saw the library where the property records were kept; the billiard room (the table an acre of faded green baize, the faded lampshades above it tilted and broken); a couple of sitting rooms; a bar, probably once a butler's pantry but now like something from a 1970s beer commercial; the backstairs for the long-gone servants; and sundry utility rooms beyond the kitchen. But under Janet's reign the grand old house was trying its hardest to be a cosy family home, and photos of her kids and grandkids jostled for prominence on every available surface. On the walls were numerous execrable abstract paintings done by Janet, all huge and all red, mixed in with what I was sure were important Australian artworks, but the tour proceeded at such a clip there was no time to look. Everywhere I glanced there was a hotchpotch of good stuff and rubbish, all in different stages of neglect. And so much furniture. Because the rooms were so large. Even the bathroom across the hall from my bedroom could have been measured in acres. The shower, the bath, the toilet and the pedestal wash basin stood at lonely distances far apart. The white shower stall (cavernous) was stained orange with rust. A clear plastic mat, which was mouldy underneath, was provided to stand on. Mercifully, the shower curtain, also mouldy, hung arms-lengths away. The ceiling there, as elsewhere, was about 6 metres high: impossible to clean or fix easily where it was dirty and broken. I thought of Janet's grandchildren who, when they all piled in to visit at Christmastime, must racket around the house, simultaneously thrilled and repelled by all they saw, noticing every detail and strangeness. I imagined them in the bath, wide-eyed.

Despite numerous drinks in the alcove by the stairs, Janet effortlessly produced a lovely little evening meal of marinated chicken; though she was impatient with the broccolini by the time she got to it, giving it repeated hurry-up stabs, knife into the pot, as it boiled. She had little candles dotted around the kitchen table at which we sat; and there was more wine and ice cream later. She didn't ever ask would I like this or that, she just put things in front of me in a confident, generous way—a countrywoman provider, though on the genteel end of the scale. We talked easily about the pioneering years and the consolidation of the property, its vastness in the golden days when several brothers and their families occupied the mansion, making sense of all those rooms that now only Janet rattled around in. There were tales of lean years and learning the land; digressions on this family member or that who went away, came back, made a fortune in finance, was the country's leading expert in rose growing, dug silage pits to save the place from drought, was tough but fair; there was gossip about city apartments and duties in town, about prominent neighbours and famous visitors.

In the morning I was prickle-eyed from lack of sleep and slightly hungover, but Janet was fresh. She insisted on driving me around on a quick tour of the property's nearest buildings. There was a beautiful old shearing shed (good for parties for the kids, Janet said), there was a schoolhouse, a family chapel, several original cottages, the property's own store.

And then, at last, I was released. I climbed into the Camry and headed home.

I'd had a good time. Janet was excellent company and we'd had many laughs; she was a kind woman. But as I drove off I had a better appreciation of the complexities of living with history. Everything in that house had the strings of its provenance attached, and the same would be true outside for every paddock and every windmill and trough. I could absolutely understand the impulse if the next inheritor wanted to walk away, to start living on new terms. The place was an encumbrance, built on something false. It was telling that, in all our discussion, the topic of how Janet's family first took their land was never raised, by either of us.

I powered off down the road: a beautiful day, sublime countryside. And as I turned my head to look out the driver's-side window, there it was: a smell, faint but distinct. Rat on my cardigan.

•

This pleasant hillock. Who wouldn't choose to sit down here?

After Georgia and I have finished our sweaty work, I roll the mower back in under the house. Most times I have a smile of satisfaction on my grimy face. The job is done. The little house made nice. Thank you, I say into the dry air under the house, to the people who brought the shells. And when I look beyond the mower to the cockles which dot away into the darker reaches, it seems weirdly right that the fibro scraps are also there. It's fucked up and apt at the same time. The all of it is evidence that can't be dodged.

That is what I learnt from my visit to Janet. And from Georgia, who was admired for her clear-eyed personal honesty, and the honesty of her writing, and whose forthrightness I'm always reminded of in the forthright act of mowing.

It is wrong to dodge the truth. And ultimately futile.

My home is set on an asbestos-contaminated midden.

That frankness is the only thing I have to offer back to the shell-gatherers.

What does that phrase, 'asbestos-contaminated midden', mean to me? To me it represents all the complications of our settlement history, all the messes that can never be undone or neatly separated out. The asbestos, the rat: they are symbols of the old, careless white fouling of the nest and white despoil, which has ongoing ramifications for us all. It cannot be pretended away. It happened.

The shells, well, it might seem strange to say, but they make me happy. They are a sign of life. They link me to humanity across time. Through them I make contact. From these very cockles and whelks—the ones right here—mothers and fathers and children once picked the meat and slurped it down.

With the mower parked, I go around to the front yard to admire my work. There's no footpath, so the grassed nature strip (ironic term!) rises up to merge into the low hill on which the house is set. It looks especially good in the late afternoon, when the lawn's undulations are given dimension by a mix of shadow and sun.

Though it might be a culturally misguided gesture on my part (built on a notional folly convenient to myself), I mow for all of us: for Georgia, and my family, and for the first people and their families. A well-maintained lawn has long been a sign in suburbia of a household's overall order and good health, and so it pleases me to tend these grounds. The grassy knoll must be kept inviting.

In openness we are better off.

Self-portraits

I'm running a test. On the gear I've hired. I pull the curtains together and shut the door to make the afternoon room as dark as possible. I've got a video camera set up on a tripod at the foot of the queen-sized bed I sleep in in the house up the coast. An infrared light is clamped to the top of the wardrobe door, which I've wedged ajar with a chair. Power boards and cables run over the floor. I open the viewfinder of the Sony camera. Information appears, but the picture behind it is grainy. I look for a button on the camera that the guy in the hire place showed me. There it is, marked NIGHTSHOT. The word instantly appears on the screen and the picture of the bed is suddenly crisp monochrome with an overall green cast. I grab a nearby shirt and wave it in front of the infrared light while straining to also keep sight of the viewfinder. It's the only way I can think of to check the light's working properly, and where it's pointing. The human eye can't see infrared. That's how come you can sleep with it on. The shadow of the flopping shirt crosses the pillows, so everything seems okay. Later, lying in bed that night, I will see a science fiction cluster of red dots in the glass of the small lamp aiming blankly at me. Twenty red dots, to be precise. (The next morning I get up and count them.) No glow emanates from them. Twenty dull red dots aiming blankly at me.

Everything's set.

A last glance at the viewfinder. How odd. In that confined area of sunken green, I intend to put myself.

•

When I began writing personal essays it was never my intention to blurt out a lot of autobiographical details, but once I'd written a few I realised that, cumulatively, some kind of portrait would inevitably emerge. That got me interested in the idea of investigating painted self-portraits and commentary about them. It also made me wonder what I might find if I looked more deliberately at myself. In fact, when I realised that many of my essays were about looking, it seemed only fair to look more directly at myself. That's when I came up with the idea of filming myself asleep and doing a day of selfies.

I would film myself over consecutive nights while I slept

(the first night in wide shot, the second in close-up), and throughout the intervening day take a photo of myself every fifteen minutes. This would be done up the coast at the holiday house. It would give me a cache of material about myself, awake and asleep, over a particular period in time. With it I might examine myself: perhaps to construct a self-portrait; perhaps to more closely investigate myself as an artist-writer.

What would I see if I could see something of the usually unseeable me, the outside me, the me that was otherwise not knowable to myself? I'd never been much interested in the appearance of my walking-around body, being too busily engaged looking and thinking outwards from behind its eyes. But now I had a good reason to boomerang that gaze and an objective framework in which to do it. I didn't want to make any advance guesses as to what I'd find, nor did I want my behaviour in front of the camera to be self-conscious and taint the outcome. Hence so many selfies. By turning them into a chore I'd bore myself into being unself-conscious—although, to be honest, it's probably an understatement to say I have no natural inclination towards posing. The selfies would provide a full record of me in the course of a day and perhaps I'd accidentally catch hold of a hitherto-veiled aspect of my person. Secretly I didn't expect to get much from them, but it was hard to be as neutral over the sleep component of the experiment. That idea, when I first thought of it, immediately seemed recklessly thrilling. Sleep is such a fascinating realm, and the thought of being able to visit ourselves while we are disappeared in it is at once compelling and unsettling. Notionally, I intended to cross a boundary and go where, in nature, I did not belong. Just to question the state, which we customarily take for granted, seemed somehow subversive. Is it not strange that come nightfall we obediently take ourselves off, en masse, to lie down like grubs? To the nightly hiatus we surrender, in our dormitories vulnerable and soft, at the mercy of any who would open a window, pick a lock, light a match.

To regenerate, we have no choice but to plug into sleep, and yet, while rationality rests from leadership, who are we? In the dwelling place of dreams and sexuality, who are we and how do we behave?

•

Weeks before any filming took place I did my usual thing and went on a research binge. I got hold of a pile of art books and then I went to the Art Gallery of New South Wales. From room to room I roamed, armed with an incomplete list of the self-portraits currently hanging, but I wondered if they would be easy to identify anyway. My art books tell me the 'look' of self-portraits is commonly one of mastery, containment, self-possession. It may even tend to the imperious—the artist presenting themselves as creator and controller of mini-worlds. Because artists often paint themselves from a mirror, a strange feedback loop can occur which does not happen in other portraits. The eyes of the artist bore into the surface of the mirror: the looker endlessly looking at the looker. But another thing happens too: the viewer, in standing in front of the artist's portrait, replaces the mirror, setting up the possibility of a conceptual swap, whereby the viewer may 'become' or 'enter' the artist. In looking, both the artist and the viewer might glimpse some truth about the artistic personality with its gift for 'insight', or something important about art itself.

As it turned out, at the gallery it *was* pretty easy to pick a self-portrait. While there were some detached works where the artists seemed only to be asking, *What form do I take as an object and how does the light fall on me?*, the majority had an unmistakable intensity about them. An air of isolation clung to these sitters. Self-possession did indeed seem common. This was sometimes depicted as determination, and occasionally as full-blown defiance. There was wariness and weariness. There was melancholy. Most subjects looked prepared to give whatever their vocation asked of them, even while expecting it would never be enough or serve to much good.

Two portraits in the gallery stood out. One by Sidney Nolan and the other by Margaret Preston. In both, as in a multitude of self-portraits, the subjects hold palette and brushes, an identifying cliché you'd think artists would want to avoid, but important of course as the mediating tools they use to communicate with the world. It's the way they are held that's interesting—almost always between the artist's body and the viewer, and acting as a kind of demarcation or barrier between the artist and the world. Sometimes the palettes and brushes obviously look like shields and weapons, but weapons deployed for self-defence rather than attack.

In the Nolan picture (*Self Portrait*, 1943), the artist is daubed with war paint. Gallery notes say that at the time of painting he was a soldier in the army, and a year later he went AWOL, but to me that's only incidentally relevant. There's far more going on. Nolan's china blue eyes are hurt and questioning. Dominating the foreground are brushes spiking out of a palette. Like the look in Nolan's eyes, the brushes actually work in two directions—going *into* and *out of* the painting. They resemble arrows stuck in a target but fired with the aim of piercing the artist; and, at the same time, they look to be tools of resistance parried outwards in defence.

In her self-portrait of 1930, Margaret Preston is apparently serene. She wears a black dress and stands in front of a pink brick wall. Her equipment is rendered in subdued tones and naturalistically. There is nothing aggressive about them: as objects they make no comment. Nevertheless, the way Preston holds them squarely in front of herself keeps her at a slight remove from the viewer. Her black dress is very plain and strong. In fact, she looks as if she is ministering, as if she has just come from a funeral to a home where a wake will be held. Instead of the priest's ritual equipment of Bible and chrism, she has brought palette and brushes. They are the necessary accoutrements of her office, but as a professional she knows not to expect them to deliver truths which are a comfort to others. Preston's clear-eyed gaze passes the viewer's left shoulder to fix on something beyond. She will be calm and pleasant at the wake but hold herself apart from the emotions of others. She understands, as they don't, that art, like death, cannot be swayed from its overall impersonal course. Its terms must be accepted and 'got through'.

•

CLICK.

At 6.36 am I wake and immediately reach for my phone to take the first of what will be 113 selfies. (If you're thinking the maths doesn't work, you're right—sometimes I took extras by mistake.)

I get up and stop the video. I remove the camera from the tripod and hook it up to my laptop to download the entire night's worth of vision. The download takes a geological age. Which is nerve-racking. It's been a bother sorting out the technical side of this experiment given the low light conditions, the time span, battery life and file size, so when the transfer is finally complete it's a massive relief.

While it's tempting to break out the popcorn and settle in for an extended viewing session, I don't. I've got another night to go before I have to take back the gear, and I want to save up my viewing impressions. I restrict myself to a quick check: there I am in my nightie climbing into bed; jump to the end of the vision; there I am at dawn climbing out.

I'm wearing a nightie because I always do. I gave up caring if it was daggy in my late twenties when I realised I hated sleeping naked: I get too cold. I suppose if I was naked it might add something to the experiment, because there I would be, basic and animal; literally exposed if I kicked off the covers. But it's not the usual me and it might change my behaviour, and that's something I'm trying to avoid.

Intermittently the timer goes off on the phone. Another selfie. Snap.

With the successful capture of the night's vision, I suddenly feel good. Really good. Too good to stay inside. It worked! I'm the sort of happy that, on an unseasonably hot, windless autumn day, needs to go walking for three hours. TIMER-SELFIE-CLICK. I throw a few things into a backpack, including a selfie-stick, and head off up to the ridge and the national park, determined to go all the way to Tallow Beach. There won't be too many more days left like this before winter comes and I can't let this one be lost.

•

High up on the ridge the orange dirt of the fire trail ribbons out in front of me and behind. Low scrubby trees and coastal heath give way to views on my left of the ocean and to views on my right of the estuary; sometimes both at once. This is the summit of my place. The estuary, cradled between steep bushy hills, is in many ways my cradle, the childhood arena of family holidays, loved for its wharves and its fish and its tides. It's where I learnt to look as a kid. In adult life, also on holidays, I have come to know the beach, the coarse grain of the sand, salmon riding in the walls of waves, salt misting the headland come late afternoon. Up here on the ridge I straddle the two parts of myself: the one enclosed and kept close; the other that wants no constraint and will not conform.

This would be a good spot to scatter the cremated gravel of my bones.

The timer goes off on the phone. So far I've pretty much been randomly adjusting the length of the selfie stick when I snap pictures so I'll appear sometimes closer and sometimes further away. I don't care how I look, or about the background, or even how the photos turn out technically. I haven't posed once, but this time I intend to, because I've just stepped up onto a rock and seen my destination below. I've never set foot on Tallow Beach before—so strange that in all these years I've never made the effort to go the extra way there.

Only then does it occur to me that I'm breaking the terms of my experiment in quite a major way: I'm about to do something out of the ordinary, something I've never done before. But actually it's entirely fitting as another expression of my inquiry into the unknown—and proof that I don't like being told what to do, even by me.

I take a picture of myself pointing down to the beach, in the end not striking a valiant attitude, but one that shows me to be cheesed off. I've noticed specks moving around down on the sand and I'm saying: *There! I'm going all the way down there and still there will be PEOPLE! Urrgh!*

The outrage in the pose is mock but the impulse behind it is genuine. I'm disappointed. I presumed I'd have the whole place to myself and now the outing is slightly spoilt. The unknown isn't so unknown if it's known by other people. I'll have to skulk around avoiding the PEOPLE, and in doing so miss out on seeing that end of the beach. Gone will be the wholesale feeling of wildness I hoped to have when there alone.

As I turn to leave my ridge-top eyrie, I catch a glimpse of the phone's screen. The camera app is still open but the selfie mode has automatically reverted to the normal setting. For a half-second I see my shadow, thrown forward on the platform of sandstone on which I've been standing.

Though it's not on my schedule, I stop and take the shot, because I recognise that looming, over-tall shadow, cut off at the shins. It's the main character out of my failed colonial baroque novel. He also walks alone in nature. Because he wishes, and because he has no choice.

In one way I'm not that surprised to see him here. This is exactly the kind of place he'd like to be in.

•

The road down is steep *and* undulating, and strewn with small stones which roll like ball bearings under my shoes. I have to take short steps and go slow. But I don't care. It doesn't matter how long it takes to get there. This outing can be whatever it is for as long as it wants; there's nothing and no one I have to check in for. And that restores my relaxed and expansive mood after the unwelcome intrusion of PEOPLE.

When the road levels at the bottom I take a track through the tea-tree down to the beach. After the trees, but before the beach proper, the path opens onto a flat area of tufty grasses and low-to-the-ground, wind-wizened bushes. Exquisite, obdurate things, variously hard-prickled. If you could bear to grab a handful and close your fist on them, through the pain you'd feel the full glory of their stubbornness. TIMER-SELFIE-CLICK. Great exhalations of salty breath come off the surf, which powers in.

The PEOPLE are at the northern end of the beach—jumping around. I turn south. Make for the point, there to sit on a rock and eat my apple lunch.

CLICK. One cheek bulging with apple.

•

There are obvious reasons why artists may choose to paint a self-portrait. To use themselves as a model when no other is available. To advertise their skills. To record their own likeness for posterity—perhaps as a way of achieving a kind of immortality, or at least to thwart mortality. To present a 'true' self, the inward self, the creating self, a desired self, a reviled self, an alter ego (think Grayson Perry). The traditional use of a mirror no doubt encourages thinking about doubles and replicas. Doppelgängers.

Doppelgänger: from the German words 'double' and 'walker' or 'goer'.

The *Encyclopaedia Britannica* says: 'double goer'; in

German folklore, 'a wraith or apparition of a living person, as distinguished from a ghost'.

•

The apple tastes good. As I munch I see a little goat path which goes up and around the rocks behind me. It might lead all the way to Box Head, where the estuary opens to the sea. A marked national parks' trail on the ridge top is the official way there, but this absconder's route, clinging to the hillside, appeals. It's impossible to resist the lure to at least see around the first point, where surely there'll be no more PEOPLE.

CLICK.

The path leads first to Little Beach, a sandy nip between the curved embrace of rocks. I take a scenery photo while I'm there, despite reckoning the beauty marred by the graffiti somebody has painted on a big rock in the middle of the beach. Later, when I look properly at the photo, my dismay at that incursion is replaced with a smile. The lime green symbol on the rock is no scribble. Its position is strategic (the ocean spreads out behind it), and it is well and carefully executed. It's a single, wide-open eye, with long eyelashes. A third eye. Only via the photo was its mad and entirely coincidental relevance to my project made apparent. The hippie universe was looking back at me to throw in its own comment.

Behind the beach the track goes past a natural spring which leaks out of a tannin crease in the land. From there it becomes a contour line, winding around an exposed hillside, whereupon it further narrows. To the width of a human foot. But I feel good going on, aware now of a strange but comfortable presence. Up ahead, just out of sight, someone is confidently walking on. At first I am happily puzzled, then just happy when it comes to me who it is. My doppelgänger.

Around another bend, with the end still not in sight, the path becomes such a thin dirt thread and so precarious, it's hard to know what sort of creature could use it without falling into the sea. I have no choice. I must stop. But the figure from my baroque novel walks on, for the time being at least, without me.

•

To 'see' (and therefore *understand*) something others don't, the creative ego must take a solitary journey.

The journey is often styled as a visit to the underworld; as if, in order to realise a new thing, the artist must make it from the anti-matter found in a place of disembodiment and shadows. The journey entails risk: the traveller might experience terrible things that cannot be forgotten, they might lose themselves for a time. They might not return at all. The unique thing the artist brings back is the reward for stepping outside safe boundaries.

But there are no guarantees. Will the effort have been worthwhile for what is produced? And how will what is produced be received? The thing retrieved might be something beautiful or heretical—or ephemeral; the artist does not know before they set out and doesn't always get to choose.

Art historian Joseph Leo Koerner says: 'Melancholic and estranged, the artistic ego, turned inward and against itself, becomes the object of personal and social *sacrifice*: personal sacrifice through single-minded devotion to its calling; and social sacrifice, due to its being perennially misunderstood.'

The self-portrait painter unavoidably gives expression to these issues and the mixed feelings to which their vocation gives rise. They may ask how art acts on their person; and what is this strange, animating force that gives them such purpose, but which causes trouble and pain?

Inevitably, the artist must also wonder how they would live *without* art, and who they'd be then. At a moment's notice, or by long-drawn-out means, art might desert them. Bereft, abandoned: the spectre of that person haunts them.

•

TIMER-SELFIE-CLICK. I go home, click, read, click, write up my art-book notes, click. I go for a mini-walk to the extension wharf, I shower, I make dinner, eat, click, click, click-click, click.

The last shot of the day is of me standing outside the open doorway to the bedroom, with the bed in the background. CLICK.

Tonight I will sleep again for another seven or eight hours of videoing. The close-up this time.

I shut the bedroom door. Turn off the bedside lamp. Small in the high left-hand corner of the watching dark: twenty red dots.

•

In the morning, while I transfer the new sleep footage, I write up the dreams I can recall from the past two nights. Though it's hard to see what use they'll be, it seems best to note them just in case, when I'm looking through the vision, I see disturbances which look like dream activity. If I make some distinctive movements or talk in my sleep, maybe I can match them up.

Usually I don't dream much, or not that I remember, so I'm quite surprised to be able to write down four in all. While they are very different in setting, ranging from a frozen landscape to a hotel lobby, one thread is amusingly common. In each dream I am resistant to authority: mildly but firmly refusing to obey, or repeatedly putting my case when ignored—even when threatened by a third party to desist, 'or else'. In one I am pursued across sparsely treed snowfields by two soldiers on state-of-the-art snowmobiles. The soldiers should be intimidating—not just because of their machines, but because they wear black samurai armour. Their task is to arrest me. But I'm not worried. They won't stop me. At modest speed, across the snow, on my inferior contraption, I motor off.

•

Next I pack up the camera gear. I find myself doing it fondly, even reluctantly. As I've mentioned elsewhere, I used to be a TV camera operator—in the 1980s; it was my first real job—and though I haven't done that work for decades, the equipment has felt pleasingly familiar in my hands. On my first day up here, when I attached the camera to the head of the tripod, I instinctively reached underneath to level it, and yes, there it was, the nut to loosen the head, and yes, there it was, the spirit level bubble. Rock the bubble into the black circle it belongs in and lock it off.

As I pack up now I drop the legs of the tripod efficiently. Like an old pro. Like the old pro it's hard to believe I ever was. A me that's so long gone, and yet a me that my body still remembers.

I'm about to shut the lid on the camera box but at the last second I obey my hands. They want to hold the camera one more time. They know they might not get the chance to hold as good a one again and they want to take it and make it move.

I scoop it up, power on the viewfinder, press record. Steady,

I hold the floating frame and I walk it through the house to show it every room. Let this be a record. Here's how this dear house looked on this sunny day, the ninth day of April in the year 2018.

I show it every wall, lingering on those where maps of the estuary hang. I show it the floors and the furnishings. Here's the backyard, too, with its clothesline strung between two posts, here's what you see when you're sitting on the outside dunny with the door open. Here's where the car's parked (my 1998 Toyota Camry) under the overhanging bough of next-door's jacaranda. Here's the grassy knoll out the front which looks so fine when it's mowed, here's the road, here's the bay. All of this is the background to the portrait of me.

I'm giving it all to the camera. Take it in your frame and keep it from Time, which moment by moment wants to replace it with something else.

•

I transfer the vision and load the car and go. In the city, I stay just long enough to return the gear to the hire place, then I head straight back up the coast.

This afternoon I will look at all my selfies and, finally, the night footage.

•

Painting throughout its history has served many purposes, has been flat and has used perspective, has been framed and has been left borderless, has been explicit and has been mysterious. But one act of faith has remained a constant from palaeolithic times to cubism, from Tintoretto . . . to Rothko. The act of faith consisted of believing that the visible contained hidden secrets, that to study the visible was to learn something more than could be seen at a glance. Thus paintings were there to reveal a presence behind an appearance—be it that of a Madonna, a tree, or, simply, the light that soaks through a red.

John Berger said that.

•

The chequerboard of the 113 thumbnails of the selfie day fills my computer screen, beginning in grainy near-darkness with the first photo, taken almost the moment I pulled out of sleep.

I find I am older-looking than I thought. My face is permanently sleep-pushed from my habit of lying heavily on one side. This pulls the right eye socket down. In some photos this is quite marked and echoes a boxer's, slanted and puffy. The asymmetrical face can appear worn out and even sad, but when there's a hint of a smile playing in my brown eyes, a sharpness switches on. I look better when I'm wearing my reading glasses. They hide the plasticine extremes of the face, which include the deep, dark-ringed eye sockets I've always had. Prematurely, my throat is starting to lizard. And when my mouth is open my capped tooth at the front is obviously whiter than the others. It's something that people who know me well will have forgotten, but that a little kid would notice and ask a parent about later. My hair, which has recently been cut shorter than I've worn it in a while, is a messy, dyed-blonde seagull's nest; sometimes a thick strand hangs over a corner of my glasses.

In all of the pictures, when I'm not in my Kmart nightie, I'm wearing shorts and a sleeveless shirt.

Gorgeous. But an assessment of attractiveness was never the point. The fact is I'm ageing, and not very well. But as I flick through the pics, I see some where suddenly, in the right light, without any prior tending or preening at all, youth is magically restored. I am pathetically grateful for them. Oh, she's still there! The me I better recognise, the more vital one that better matches the me of my mind. Within the course of a day, both these outward selves must come and go, randomly showing themselves to others, while I, of course, have no idea whose turn it is to be in charge.

So much for my appearance.

What do I learn of my character?

It's hard to say. Probably not much. Because of the task, and because I'm not posing and therefore not animated or smiling much, because of my keen brown eyes and the one eyebrow higher than the other, I do tend to look like a person who by nature likes to look intently. This seems especially so when I flick through the photos fast, because my eyes are the one consistent anchor point in each picture. Behind that intent look is sometimes something smart, indicating a mix of curiosity and scepticism. Quite often there's a hint of amusement or relish at something quizzical. Sometimes amusement is tempered by a touch of melancholy, of self-contained acceptance of . . . what? . . . Of the facts. The facts of what? . . . The fact of the existence of complications.

Among my 113 photos, the closest I get to accidentally replicating the feedback loop of the painter's mirror is in one that's an extreme close-up. It was taken inside the house but you'd hardly know it: the background is mostly burnt-out white light from the long-room windows. I'm wearing my reading glasses and in each lens there's a small rectangular reflection of the lit phone screen. These tiny, white, transparent reflections sit over my brown irises. The face is calm, but the 'look' in those eyes is indeed that of someone trying to intently locate a place that will give something back.

•

'The quest of the self-portrait is to find something out about art.'

I said that.

It reminds me of what I came to think about the baroque period, after researching it for my novel. The baroque, I decided, pulls out all the stops trying to give you every single thing art could possibly offer, and yet it fails; because there's some pure thing at the heart of art that can't be wholly communicated, it can only be glimpsed in parts. The baroque wants to wrench that core thing from its socket and triumphantly hand it over. But it's not possible. This, I concluded, is the real message the baroque has for us. It can't be done.

In the history of art, the subject of art itself is an inexhaustible topic. What is art? What does it tell us? Where is it?

John Berger's statement about art's pledge to deliver the secrets embedded in the visible was made in a piece he wrote about Jackson Pollock. He said of Pollock:

Jackson Pollock was driven, by a despair which was partly his and partly that of the times which nourished him, to refuse this act of faith: to insist, with all his brilliance as a painter, that there was nothing behind, that there was only *that which was done to the canvas on the side facing us*. This simple, terrible reversal, born of an individualism which was frenetic, constituted the suicide.

The suicide he refers to there is the suicide of Pollock's art.

Within or beyond Pollock's pictures, Berger says, '. . . there is nothing. Only the visual equivalent of total silence.'

•

After the selfies, I watch the night footage. No one else will ever see it but me.

In the green swimming pool of the NIGHTSHOT I put myself to bed. The covers rustle as I flip the thick doona lengthways over to the other side of the bed: it's too hot for now. The white sheet and the cream thermal blanket over it will suffice. They sculpt closely to me as I turn onto my right side facing the middle of the bed, eyes shut, legs bent; my form the stylised shape of a Pompeii body.

I seem to fall asleep immediately. I do not move.

I'm watching in real time and the longer I watch myself not moving, the more the silence of the room builds to become something distinctly uncomfortable. In the quiet of my stasis, time stretches and stretches, and swells and swells, to become a controlling atmosphere that owns the night. To keep watching is unbearable: I slide through the vision to speed it up. Finally, I move in the bed, after more than an hour.

Over both nights, my sleep follows the same pattern: I go to sleep quickly and sleep soundly for long stretches, mostly only disturbed by temperature changes. If I get up and go to the toilet, I fall back to sleep quickly. Throughout the night I hardly make a sound: I don't snore (although I know I do sometimes because I've been called out at it in front of the television); twice I hear myself fart—loud and comfortable. I cannot see when I'm dreaming, although sometimes in the close-ups I think I can detect REM flickers under the eyelids, but it's hard to be sure. In the green light my skin is uniformly pale and smooth.

Only when you look very carefully can you see my breaths move the bedclothes where they cover my chest. Otherwise I sleep so peacefully you would not know I was alive. In the wide shots, when I look at that body, I see a cicada shell. So empty does it seem of anything. It reminds me of another line of Berger's about Pollock: 'On these canvases the visible is no longer an opening but something which has been abandoned and left behind.'

In the close-ups I look like my mother. People who knew her always said so, especially as I got older. In the homogenisation of the night vision we replicate faces more than we have ever done, especially now it turns my blonde hair white like hers. But it's not just hair colour that further matches us up. It's the shapes the hair takes, the waves and strong half-curls that have re-emerged since my recent cut. I remember them from her. And when I see the back of my head I'm shocked to see that my hair springs from the crown exactly the same way as hers did when pillow-messed. It seems too intimate a thing to have noticed, an invasion of the privacy of both of us, and yet it is true. *Yo lo vi*. I saw it during her last illness. Those last long days when she withdrew into herself to cope with the pain.

She/me turns on the pillow to lie flat on her back in what is the most death-like repose of each of the nights. Sharply profiled. White-faced. In the underwater light she lies there, plainly seen. But think! In truth, thick dark covers her. Dark that fills the volume of the room.

•

I have been to the other side of the night to see myself and must report back: there's not much happening.

After watching the seventeen hours of video, the only understanding I arrive at is that I don't have any attachment at all to the person on the screen. This much is very clear. Were it not for the way that person's body remembers my mother's, I would feel entirely indifferent about her. I have no special bond with or fondness for her, nor do I find her innocent oblivion in any way special or charming. Neither do I worry for her, despite her extreme vulnerability. Even the dead-looking me in the sepulchre does not affect or disturb me. I feel nothing. And when I watch the waking self slowly returning to consciousness, I continue to feel nothing, though I recognise the ritual movements as mine and remember being inside those moments.

And the selfies? I did not catch myself unawares, I see in them no hidden thing. Nothing is revealed. What I have seen in both of my experiments is merely a body in time.

Jackson Pollock saw no hidden thing. His art was in present tense, all in the wild moment, depicting the creative energy of its making. When his energy failed, as it must, the great silence, always waiting out the back, thundered in. That is what killed *him*.

•

I watch myself wake in the pre-dawn on the second morning once again. The irises of my eyes—turned into black beads by the green cast—look glassy and very strange. A white highlight drills a pinpoint in each.

I watch myself yawn. I watch myself turn on my side, go still, and think. Remember—although the vision is crisp, that's due to the camera's NIGHTSHOT setting. In truth, it's very early, the curtains are closed and the room is still very dark. I'm thinking in the dark: I have my eyes open in the dark.

My black bead eyes flick up to the twenty dots of the infrared light; I stare. I watch me watch the red dots. The twenty red dots that seem to do nothing.

You must get out of bed.

That is the message of art.

Keep looking.

Bucket of Fish

It's an all-or-nothing strategy today. I'm using up the last bits of bait from the freezer—there wasn't much there—so I've bypassed Rileys to head straight for the Hole.

It's late autumn and this will probably be the last time I go out for a couple of months. It's getting cold, and wading out to launch the *Squid* is a chilly proposition. More to the point, the good tides are just about gone. During winter the high highs only occur at night-time.

The season has been reluctant to change, but now it's on its way: under wharves mullet huddle. Heavy with eggs and milt they wait for the next big rains to flush the estuary with fresh water and send them to sea. Next time I come back up the coast they'll be gone.

Like a shop, the afternoon is closing down. The breeze has a sharp edge to it. Only the eccentric or the foolish would be out, which explains why I'm the only one here. Though my face feels scrubbed by the cold I'm toasty enough, bundled up in a jumper and a waterproof jacket. I nearly didn't make the effort to come, but I'm glad I did. The *Squid* rides fine at anchor and the fishing's been good. Every bait I've sent down has brought up a small snapper, until it seems I've pulled up my own sunset in fish. Metallic rose-and-aqua-speckled, they gleam in my hands. So far two have been big enough to keep: plate-sized beauties.

From the treed shadow of the hillside near the bridge a sea eagle comes gliding. Must be a juvenile, because when it lowers itself in graceful stages to come close I see its plumage is black and brown. It drops in further scoops, holding air under its spanned wings to hover only 5 metres or so above the surface of the water. Though it examines the water with the perspicacity of a high court judge, it removes nothing. It's maybe 10 metres away from me, so near I can hear its curiously emasculated voice, *peep peep*, as it talks to itself.

When the eagle goes, black-toupeed terns take its place, also showing interest in the rip eddies. At mangled scraps of bait I discard, they are quick scavengers.

Bucket of Fish

It's not strictly pretty out here today: the water's browny grey and, in the last of the light, rain-bearing clouds gather. I should go soon, but I'm still pulling in snapper. I think myself down to the bottom of the Hole. In the submerged terrain of down there are myriad pink flashes. The current, like a square-dance caller, sends them one way without warning, then spins them to scatter, before summoning a swift regroup.

I look in my bucket. My two fish are quiet; a little flutter of their pectoral fins is all it takes to keep them upright in their confinement. Two are enough for dinner. I reel in my line and sit a moment. The westerly blusters in under the Rip Bridge behind me; ahead the waterway opens out towards home and the mouth of the ocean. To this watery arena I have lately brought the different parts of myself to find they do indeed fit together.

I pick up my bucket of fish, lean it against the gunwale of the *Squid*. Today I thank this place. This bucket of fish I tip into the estuary. Contents returned in a blurred whoosh of colour.

Motoring back in the near-dark with my lantern on I pass the old wharf of my childhood. The air, the colours, of water, wharf, the bush behind, thicken to become each other. I think: Did I really stand there as a little kid? Did the past really happen? What was she really like, that little girl?

I don't know what she expected out of life, but she would be glad to look up and see herself driving by in her own boat, on that stretch of water, that much is sure.

Little girl, wave to me.

I'm here.

Acknowledgements

Many texts have contributed to the writing of this book and the thinking within it. David Hockney's quotes, as they appear in my essay 'My Life and the Frame', come from *A Bigger Message: Conversations with David Hockney* by Martin Gayford, 2011. Karsten Harries' work in *The Broken Frame*, published by the Catholic University of America Press, 1989, was also helpful for that essay.

John Berger's quotes in my essay 'Self-portraits' originate in 'A Kind of Sharing' from *Keeping a Rendezvous* by John Berger, 1992. For that essay I also consulted 'Self Portraiture Direct and Oblique' by Joseph Leo Koerner, in *Self Portrait: Renaissance to Contemporary*, Anthony Bond and Joanna Woodall, published by the Art Gallery of New South Wales and the National Portrait Gallery (Great Britain), 2005.

Special thanks to Andrew Sloane for granting me permission to use his story and words in my essay 'The Nature of Words'. (*Ngayi*, Andrew.) Andrew's quotes come from an episode of 'Word Up', which aired on the ABC Radio National program *Awaye!* on 14 October 2017.

This is largely a book about family, and I have been lucky with mine. Special thanks to my siblings Di and Roger for their unfailing support. Thanks also to Pam and Patrick Clark.

I am indebted to my dear writer friends, especially Tegan Bennett Daylight, Lucinda Holdforth and Charlotte Wood. They are the best creative companions.

Thank you to Keiran Rogers, who provided early encouragement, and went out of his way to deliver it. Thanks also to Lyn Tranter, and at Allen & Unwin, Jane Palfreyman, Ali Lavau, Angela Handley and Clara Finlay.